SØRLANDET

– The Magnificent Coast of Southern Norway

SØRLANDET

– The Magnificent Coast of Southern Norway

Øivind Berg
Jan Atle Knutsen
Photographer: Øystein Paulsen
Translation by Caroline Babayan

Kom forlag

Foreword

This book is our way of presenting the South Coast of Norway – the magnificent coastline of Sørlandet. The key words for this region are summer, sun and happy holidays. Young or old, everyone simply has happy memories from a holiday in Sørlandet, and understandably visitors always come back. As residents, what we have in common with the holidaymakers is the pleasure of strolling along the beaches or sailing through the reefs and islets of the Coastal Archipelago Park.

We who have created this book genuinely love the archipelago of Sørlandet, and spend time here as often as we can. In our opinion, the experience of nature is enhanced by knowledge about what we see. A white seagull is more than just a marine bird, and it is fun to know the difference between a common gull and a great black-backed gull. And the loud screeches of the seagulls acquire a deeper meaning when we know the reason. The same applies to everything most of us do not see or hear - all that moves under the surface of the sea.

The South Coast nature is multifaceted. We have therefore been obliged to make choices concerning the subject matters. We hope that this book can contribute to deepen your experiences of nature. We believe that with more knowledge about the beauty and the quality and complexity of the nature along the Southern Coast, you will be able to enjoy it more and also be encouraged to preserve it.

We hope that our children shall be able to experience this fantastic natural environment and feel responsible for the Coastal Archipelago Park - or as we call it "The Norwegians' favourite summer place." Perhaps we will all meet out there, under the soaring sky and the warm summer sun, accompanied by seagull screeches and the splash of waves - or on a rock out in the sea one windy and icy winter day. Because Sørlandet - the Norwegian Riviera – is endlessly more that just sun and summer.

Tromøy and Fevik June 2007
Øivind Berg, Jan Atle Knutsen and Øystein Paulsen

Part I: **The Norwegians' Favourite Summer Place**

From the archipelago of Arendal

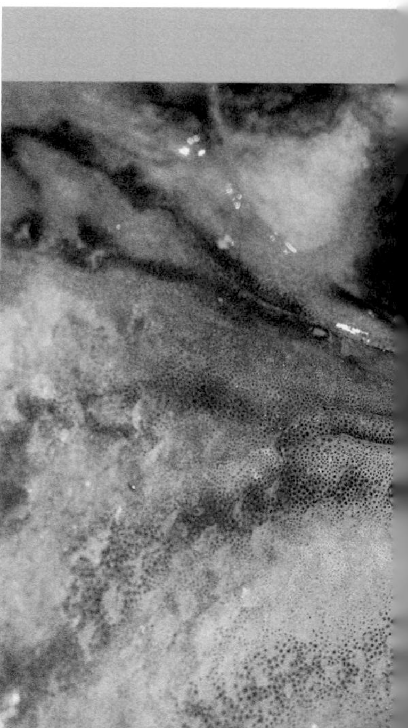

The Norwegians'

From Flatskjær east of Lyngør Lighthouse.

Favourite Summer Place

Sørlandet

The word gives pleasant associations with summer, sun, sea, swimming and relaxing holidays.

When Vilhelm Krag, in an article in 1902, suggested to call the southern part of Norway 'Sørlandet,' few people believed that the concept would become common property.

Today, the Archipelagos of Sørlandet, the coastal line of Telemark and Agder counties, which comprises many large groups of islands – is the most visited areas in Norway during the summer holidays. Therefore, many people associate Sørlandet with sun, summer and carefree holidays – the wonderful antidote to the every day hustle and bustle.

In Sørlandet you can "fritter away time." All that matters here is the calm and the freedom.

The Coastline of Sørlandet is gorgeous beautiful and spacious. There is room for all.

Welcome to the Norwegians' favourite summer destination.

"HALF OF NORWAY'S POPULATION SPEND THEIR SUMMER HOLIDAYS IN SØRLANDET"

The Joys of Boating

Counting this summer, I have sailed back and forth along my coast, in various little boats, for the last sixty two summers. Maybe I have a record in loyalty to my coast. When I write 'my coast' I don't mean it literally. I share the coast with many other people – almost everyone in the world, and do so with pleasure, with those who use it with love.

When I began this wet, drifting summers sixty-two years ago, 'my coast' was the inner Oslo fjord, from Bunnefjord to Drøbak.

My first boat was an ancient lifeboat from an unknown ship. The lifeboat had ballast made of cement and metal scrap on board, plus a mast and sails from a condemned sailing boat of unknown type and age. It leaked like a sieve every spring when we launched it, but it remained more or less afloat throughout the summer. This old, knackered leaky boat of mine had a little foredeck, and underneath I could camp with my sleeping bag and Primus burner. The boat had of course no engine, just two sturdy, heavy-duty oars.

My expeditions at that time were modest. I was an explorer in search of new countries by Nesodden, within Bunnefjord. I was very proud when I had explored Oslo's harbour basin, and ventured all the way to the other side of the fjord to unidentified and perhaps unfriendly territories. Later, I acquired a bigger and better and more habitable boat and 'my coast' became the coast of Gothenburg in Sweden to Hidra outside Flekkefjord.

Now that I have become older than my boats, my coast has once again become smaller. It starts from the south of the Koster islands in Sweden to Risør in East Agder, and once in a while, to my childhood's inner Oslo fjord.

This is the part of the Norwegian coast that I claim to know like the inside of my pocket – admittedly a somewhat exaggerated claim. I love to return and spend the night in harbours where I have been many times before. But it still happens that I find coves and islets I have never visited before, and once again feel like a daring explorer who has come upon new lands in the great oceans.

At the time when I started living in my boat for shorter and longer periods during summer, it was not a very usual thing to do. Now we are many. Several hundred thousands of people, I think, waft about – alone or with family and dog.

The boats have become bigger and better. They grow several feet each winter, and have done so for some time. Now, they are pleasant summer homes for big families. Homes with heated cabins and hot water and all, and most of them do not have a leaky deck, but are warm and dry below.

I have heard and read many explanations about why so many people want to live like this in a wet environment during summers. Some say that it comes naturally to us Norwegians. That it is in our bloods, so to speak – our heritage from our ancestors. Most of them came to this country, close to the North Pole, by boat. For a long time, the sea was the only transit route between places on the coast. Heavy objects and people were dependent on boats for transport. Moreover, the boats were necessary to catch their food.

Now we have roads everywhere, even under the water. We have bridges and trucks and bicycles and cars. And we buy the fish from the shops – gutted and boned.

Nevertheless, a surprisingly large number of people continue to use and love the coast. We continue to live in cramped and often wet and small vessels without any sensible reason, because often our summers by the coast are rainy and windy. And the seagulls scream and screech and there are only a couple of thin fibreglass walls between us and the strangers with barking dogs and crying babies. But that's how we like it.

Naturally, I haven't seen all the coasts of the world, but I've seen quite a few, and I believe that my coast is the most beautiful and friendly coast in the world. Many evenings are like dark velvet and warm and soft as a caress. Then I can lie and listen to the summer night whispering outside, and sometimes hear her chuckle and laugh a little, sounding happy. And I love her and hope that she lives forever and not become more private than she already is.

I think that my (and many others') love for the coast and my summer home is like any other love - unexplainable. Love cannot be explained. It kindles without any obvious reason, and just exists. I stopped looking for explanations a long time ago.

Odd Børretzen

Portør

Safe Harbour?

The boats are becoming increasingly larger, and many people feel that it is safer to moor in a guest harbour rather than a natural harbour in the skerries. A guest harbour has in addition services that many of the boat tourists today appreciate.

Washing machines and dryers, shower – not to mention electricity for TV, DVD players and computer games – are some of the facilities that make the guest harbours attractive.

In addition, there are the tempting varieties of activities and cultural events available in the coastal towns during summer.

Have the boaters become more urbane these last years?

Do the boaters nowadays avoid the best harbours? It almost seems like that, because people's travelling habits at sea have changed during these last years,

As the municipalities continue building attractive guest harbours and tempting holidaymakers with a wide variety of festivals, concerts and markets, increasingly more people are choosing these events rather than proximity to nature in a snug bay between islets and rocks. Earlier, you almost had to fight to get the best places in the natural harbours of the Archipelago.

Nevertheless, many people still appreciate a nice harbour in the Skerries. They know where to moor the boat safely, sheltered from the changing winds. And they know how to fill their days.

Often the day begins with a morning swim – regardless of weather – and then the coffee is ready. After a cup of coffee, you pull out the fishing nets that were set out the evening before. A long breakfast, on board or ashore, motivates you to clean the catch and prepare the day's main meal. Then the day is yours to do as you please – whether you stay one more night at the same place, or sail on to a new haven. This is an exclusive privilege when you are on boating holidays.

164

By Boat from Cottage to Cottage

There are Coastal Routes from Oslo fjord to Troms. In the South Coast the Coastal Route's stronghold is Kristiansand, with Bragdøya Coast Club as a natural prime mover and centre.

The idea behind the Coastal Route is the same as the DNT's network of cottages in the mountains, whereby the trekkers walk from cottage to cottage. The Coastal Route offers reasonable overnight stops at lighthouses or cottages and in some places you can even rent a rowing or sailing boat for simple environmentally friendly outdoor living.

The dream of cottage leisure in Sørlandet can come true via 'Kystleden,' The Coastal Route, which stretches along many parts of the coast, with cottages and lighthouses that are open to all. The thought behind the Coastal Route is to create a network of places for overnight stops along the coast, for people who travel by small boats or kayaks. The idea stems from the time when people seldom travelled for pleasure. They had an errand to do and in the hostels along the coast the travellers could rest or wait for better weather.

The Coastal Route offers the possibility to experience the skerries in an environment friendly manner – by boat and simple lodging, Most of the cottages on the coastal route can only be reached by boat, but some are also accessible to cyclists and foot tourists.

The Coastal Route project is a cooperation between The National Federation of Outdoor Recreation Councils (FL), The Coastal Association (a coastal cultural heritage organisation) and the Norwegian Trekking Association (DNT). Normally, you have to book the overnight stops through the local tourist offices or the DNT. For more information about the various offers see: www.kystled.no "The Coastal Route represents an important development within environmentally friendly outdoor activities. At the same time, it contributes in a major way to the preservation and use of cultural and historical buildings and structures along the coast," said Stein Lier-Hansen, the former secretary of state at the Ministry of the Environment, in 2004.

The Coastal Route in the south goes along Langesund fjord, Kristiansand and Søgne.
The Coastal Route in the Langesund fjord is relatively new with three overnight stops: Langøytangen lighthouse, Håøya and Sildevika ("Herring Bay").
The Coastal Route in Kristiansand is run by Bragdøya Coast Club and Mid-Agder Outdoor Recreation Council. The Bragdøya Coast Club has several rowing and sailing boats for rent. There are also boats for rent in Hellevika in Søgne. The Coastal Route in this area stretches from Randesund in the East to Vassøyene in the West. In this region there are more than seven simple overnight stops in houses or cottages.

Grønningen Lighthouse

The Summer Islands

The islands in the archipelago of Sørlandet are ideal for camping and getting close to nature. There, you are totally on your own, and you can spend your days according to your needs and your tempo.

The freedom a boat and a tent provide offers a number of opportunities. You can spend weeks enjoying island hopping, or stay in one place on 'your own islet.'

According to the Archipelago's camping rules, you can usually stay at the same place for two or three days. Some have their favourite spots and are reluctant to move. But in addition to the fact that they confiscate a spot for a longer period of time, they also deprive themselves from the experience of discovering new places. Our advice is therefore to explore the archipelago, in order to discover the qualities each new island or islet has. In this manner, you get to know the place, become familiar with the nature and in addition meet new people – because it is unlikely that you will remain alone for very long on 'your' islet.

Many places in the archipelago have toilets and rubbish bins, but fresh water is often hard to find. Therefore camping trips have to be planned with that in mind. The water you bring along is a limited resource reserved for drinking. For a few days 'on the rocks,' shower and running water can be replaced with refreshing dips in the sea and brushing teeth in saltwater.

The meals on the grass or by the water are memorable, whether you eat simply off the cutting board in your lap and sausages from the grill, or serve gourmet dishes prepared with fresh ingredients from the sea. It is incredible what you can do with a Primus cooker or with charcoals and aluminium foil. Ballan wrasse, cod and whiting, with butter and wild chives never taste any better.

Is there anything better than waking up to the sound of soft ripples, impatient screeching gulls, and sunrays that make the night dew evaporate from the tent? Camping in the summer islands gives the opportunity to take an early morning swim, and a cup of coffee, long before the day tourists arrive.

The Cottage Idyll

The Norwegian summer house, made of wood, with a red-tiled roof, windows overlooking the water and usually in just two colours – white and terracotta. This is where Norway's urban dwellers stay during their holidays. It's their second home, or belongs to a relation, or is rented from a friend.

Sixty years ago many of these coastal properties were 'on sale.' Today they are pure gold mines.

The idyllic cottages are spread along the Southern Coast. Many are in fact mansions, but in between you see summer houses that stand out, both in style and the lifestyle they represent. Some are modest cottages regularly visited by people who adore the simple coastal life – in the spirit of the author Gabriel Scott. They are not very concerned with status or busy schedules. They take one day at a time, enjoying the moments and living the good life as they see it.

Many people dream of an idyllic cottage in Sørlandet, but few are capable of realizing such a dream. Some utilise the possibilities camping provides. Camping sites by the sea were never meant as a permanent 'residence permit' on the beach. But this has also become a kind of cottage idyll along the Southern Coast.

The properties that decorate the coastal strip are mostly reserved for the wealthy, or those who have been lucky enough to inherit properties left by family members who were foresighted and understood the value these properties represented.

For less than 60 years ago, many of these properties along the coast were sold because it was impossible to live there – they could not make enough to feed a family. To buy a property by the sea for recreational purposes made the Southerners shake their heads in wonder. What a waste!

Today these costal properties have become 'gold mines' where each metre of a beach is worth millions.

Each spring, there is a debate in Norway about building cottages near the sea. Everyone has an opinion about the problems that privatisation creates, but few do anything about it. Even the building regulations in the Planning and Building Act, which forbid constructions closer than hundred meters to the coastal line, are threatened.

To the left: 'Permanent' camping huts at Skottevig Camping in Blindleia between Lillesand and Kristiansand.
To the right: Villhelm Krag's 'bay' is finely situated in Ny-Hellesund.

DVB
TracVision G4
KVH
sa zephyros

City Hubbub?

"They want idyll, but want it bloody fast!" says the local fisherman and shakes his head at the city people in streamlined boats full of horsepower and electronic equipment. But we have to acknowledge that the nostalgic boat life is a thing of the past for most of us. Even the diehards in The Coastal Route concede that they should perhaps allow people to use 'skerrie jeeps' when travelling from cottage to cottage, although the idea is to come there without engine power – only with oars and sails. This option is still available and there are those who are fascinated by it and consider it as the ultimate 'good life.'

However, many people want to have the comforts they are used to, also during their holidays. They want to be able to shift between work and play quickly – or to do their jobs while enjoying fine summer days.

In newspaper interviews, some boat tourists have described what they consider to be the best part of a boating holiday in Sørlandet. The answers are varied: The children on board appreciate the short distance from the harbour to the DVD rental or the cinema. Mum and the youngsters are excited about the shopping possibilities in the small towns and "the labelled articles on sale everywhere!"

Probably these interviews reflect what the boat tourists are concerned with there and then, and that the situation is different when they are on their way. Hopefully, most people slow down, turn off the engine, the CD and DVD players, and anchor in a sheltered bay, far away from the city hubbub – with just the sound of the sea birds and the waves, and the wonderful scent of saltwater and seaweeds.

Modern lifestyle and culture take over places far from the city's clamour and commotion. What happens to us when the city noises stretch beyond the remotest reefs? Do we bring with us the restlessness and stress, or do we manage to let go and enjoy the freedom the cosy skerries provides for us?

Transformer station in bitmap graphics. Artwork by Alfred Vaagsvold at Lista Lighthouse west of Farsund.

We may call it an "unplugged experience" with naked, raw nature and music, when Canal Street Jazz and Blues festival in Arendal invites to Lighthoue jazz in Little Torungen outside Arendal, in the last week of July. This is probably one of the most urbane events one can imagine in the skerries during the summer holidays.

The contrast from the dim clubs to the majestic nature of Skagerrak is enormous – both for the artists and the audience. This is an unusual and alluring decibel input among the seabirds, biting stonecrops and an armada of holiday boaters. You need a boat if you want to experience music at a lighthouse far out in the archipelago – with the sun-down breeze as chorus and the rocks and reefs as the amphitheatre.

One by-product of the influx of this city culture in the archipelago is, of course, that increasingly more people discover the beauty of the place – with or without musical accompaniment.

Concert at Lille Torungen outside Arendal.

Amassalik
EXPLORER

Kayaking in the Skerries

The coastline of Sørlandet is a paradise for sea kayaking. Hardly any other vehicle is better suited for exciting exploration of the archipelago than kayak.

The broad and fine archipelago in Sørlandet provides good paddling conditions within the lee of islets and rocks.

With a kayak you can glide soundlessly through the waters, smoothly drifting forward, even in very shallow water. This enables you to explore narrow straits and bays, bringing you fascinatingly close to the bird life. It seems almost like the birds are not afraid of the kayak paddling softly and silently past them.

These last years, interest in paddling has increased enormously in Norway. And each year more people discover the sport, both as a recreation and as training. The best paddling periods are probably before and after the general staff holiday, because during the holidays the boat traffic is quite congested in the middle of the day. And it can often feel downright unsafe to be in a kayak at sea.

Many boaters drive fast and do not pay much attention to their surroundings. Some are not aware of the consequences of making big waves behind the boat, because they seldom look around. For kayakers and other people in small boats such situations can be directly dangerous. If you choose to paddle early in the morning, or a little later in the evening, you can avoid these dangers, and you can enjoy the Archipelago's peaceful silence and calm – even in the middle of the holidays.

In May, June and actually also towards the end of August and during September you can have the skerries all to yourself.

It can also be fascinating to paddle on clear autumn days and even during winter. When it is cold in the water, a wetsuit is a good insurance and make sure you choose fine and windless days. Paddling along the shoreline provides extra security.

Betweeen Portør and Levangsbukta there are paddling routes very few people know about, making them perhaps more fascinating. This coastline can be very difficult to explore by boat, because there are rocks and reefs on every corner. Kayaking, on the other hand, is perfect, because the route follows the shore and it is not long - perfect for a pleasant day trip during summer.

Set out in Portør early in the morning and head south, keeping to the inner side of the islets and rocks, to Levangsbukta, which lies a couple nautical miles from Portør. You have to cross a few small open areas, but the paddling trip through the inner parts of Larholmen and past Grytodden via Bruntangen to Levangsbukta is manageable for most people with a little paddling experience. In the afternoon, you can paddle back with the southwest wind behind you.

Sørlandsleia, part of the coastal areas of Tvedestrand and Arendal, are also good for paddling. The best route is to start in Sagesund, paddle through the beautiful Furøya, out of Oksefjord and in to Eikeland fjord on the inner side of Tverrdalsøya towards Kilsund. The trip continues on the inner side of Flosterøya towards Arendal.

Biting stonecrop

The Coastal Archipelago Park

Preserved for Outdoor Recreation

The work to preserve the Archipelagos of Sørlandet as a Coastal Archipelago Park, named "Skjærgårdsparken", was initialized in 1973/74, by the newly established Ministry of the Environment. The idea behind the archipelago project was to permanently preserve areas of the coastal nature and organize them for public utilisation and recreation.

The Ministry of the Environment has now taken the initiative to fullfill the work by establishing a Coastal Park also in the Lyngdal, Farsund, Kvinesdal and Flekkefjord municipalities. This work began in 2006, and will probably be fulfilled in 2008. The goal is to have a continuous coastal archipelago park from Grenland to Åna Sira – to cover the coast of Telemark, Aust-Agder and Vest-Agder counties.

"PRESERVED PERMANENTLY FOR THE GENERAL PUBLIC"

For the Poor and the Rich

Today, the Coastal Archipelago Park of Sørlandet consists of more than 650 recreation areas situated on islands, islets and the mainland coast from Langesund to Lindesnes.

The safeguarded areas in the Coastal Park is permanently secured with free access to all – regardless of position and status. These recreation areas are generally secured through legal agreements between the landowners and the Ministry of the Environment, or through state or municipal purchase.

According to these agreements, the private owners still own the Archipelago Park areas, but can only use it for traditional, environment-friendly agriculture. The State, on behalf of the general public, have paid for specified rights to public use and to set up buoys, toilets, rubbish bins and information boards, etc.

The right of free access to nature is part of our cultural heritage. According to the Outdoor Recreation Act, the "everyman's right", is a term describing the general public's right to access uncultivated land for recreation, regardless of permissions and ownership. The wilderness is described as uncultivated land and includes most waterways, beaches, moors, woods, and mountains. Arable land is cultivated land, pastures, meadows, cultivated pastures, gardens, plantations, farms, and building sites, in other words areas where public access will be an unwarranted disturbance for the owner or user. Because of this right of access, the "everyman's right", most of our coastal nature areas will be freely accessible without any form of protection or preservation. On the other hand, the areas of the Coastal Park that are safeguarded according to the above mentioned agreements are further expanded and developed for outdoor recreation.

Biting stonecrop grows in the outmost coastal areas from Kragerø to Trondheim fjord

Ryvingen south of Fevik.

Nature Reserves

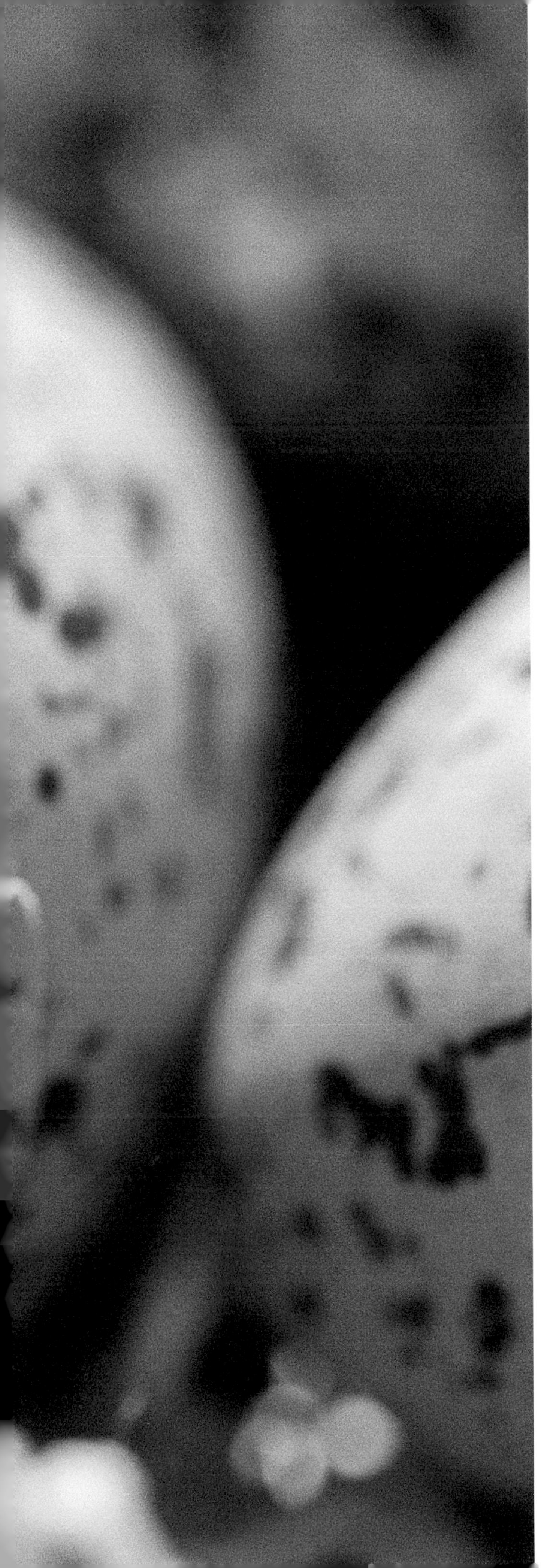

We have a number of areas in the Southern Coast that are protected according to the Nature Conservation Act. Nature reserves are the most strictly protected in Norwegian environment protection laws, and their main intention is to shelter areas with special natural landscape or fauna and flora, such as liverwort, conifers, bird sanctuaries, mires, wetlands, etc. Nature reserves are established only after comprehensive documentation.

Nature monuments are special natural phenomena that have scientific or historical interest, such as geological formations or specific trees.

Everyone is welcome to roam in protected areas, but people are requested to tread carefully and mind the fauna and flora.

Note that there may be specific protection regulations for each nature reserve.

In the bird sanctuaries, meaning in areas where the birds are protected, you are not allowed to go ashore or travel through, in the period from April 15 to July 15. This prohibition also includes boating in a zone within a distance of 50 meters from land.

The County governor's department of environment has the responsibility to manage all nature reserves.

The majority of people respect the preserved areas along the Southern Coast with almost 85 seabird sanctuaries where it is forbidden to land from 15th April to 15th July.

Seagull chick, a few days old.

Egg from Eurasian oystercatcher with chick about to hatch through its shell and join the life in the Archipelago.

Development Pressure

The gradual development taking place in Southern Norway is steadily usurping larger areas of the coastal nature we all love. It is easy to protect what we see, but under the surface of the water there are many things that are invisible for the holiday makers, the boat tourists and the authorities.

Clean environment, varied natural habitats, unpolluted sea food, abundance of fish and crabs are important to us, whether we are residents or on holiday in Sørlandet. It is necessary to protect the common goods such as the beaches, the isles and the reefs. Therefore, the authorities are planning to expand the conserved areas in the Coastal Archipelago Parks. The essential question is whether these common goods are so valuable to us that we choose to prioritise nature rather than our eager development plans? Most people would root for nature if asked to give an opinion. But then there is that eternal question of theory and practice.

In these last years, we have become relatively good at conserving the natural environment on land, but conservation of the marine nature is still at an early stage.

A tennis court at the outmost end of the Archipelago.

We remain unaware when industrial pollution and sludge in our fjords are destroying the living conditions for the sugar kelp. But divers have reported that something is seriously wrong. The consequences of the disappearance of the kelp in the fjords are unknown.

Some municipalities have begun to map the biological diversity in the sea in order to take steps to preserve the natural resources. About time, many people will say. May it inspire other coastal municipalities, too!

The sugar kelp in the fjords is in serious danger. The bottom is covered by so much sludge that the spires are unable to take root. But out on coast the kelp meadows are still intact. Extreme sea water temperature during summer due to climate changes may also play some role, as the sugarkelps are put under serious stress when sea water temperature reach 21°C.

Valøyene east of Hestnes islands at Grimstad.

Cultural Landscape

Nowadays, much work is done to preserve ancient cultural landscape in the Archipealgo, particularly, areas such as small mowed meadows, pastures, beach meadows and leafy vegetations, which have characteristic biological community.

The meadows are protected in order to prevent overgrowth, either by mowing or grazing. Sometimes it is necessary to use more drastic methods to preserve the original cultural landscape, for example by burning the juniper bushes.

In many of the most popular places in the skerries, it is a tradition for the school children to clear the debris from the beaches in spring, before the summer guests arrive. This way, the children and youngsters learn to take responsibility for the nature around them, and the skerries become clean and neat.

It ought to go without saying that we clean up after ourselves when we leave a place. And it should go without saying that one is considerate when at sea in powerful boats.

Meadow geranium and goldmoss thrive in coastal landscape.

Grazing goats on Valøyene at Fevik

Traces after juniper burning in Tromlingene at Arendal.

Slipper limpet

When Did the Sea become Beautiful?

Not Only Sun and Summer

It is not that many decades ago that people began to consider the sea as beautiful – even when it was in a stormy rage and forced them to seek refuge in their safe and comfortable homes. But then they did not have to be out there. They could wait for it to calm down and the summer sun to shine.

The people on the coast – those who lived off and with the sea – had another view. For them the sea was not just beautiful – it was also dangerous and unpredictable. The sea could be generous, and it could be deadly. But it was their daily plight and they had to live with it. Therefore, they observed in wonder at the cottages that began to pop up in the most weather-beaten and windy locations – for the sake of the view.

Many cottage owners have been surprised by the intensity of the storms and the spring tide, and have in despair witnessed the damages the sea can cause when places are unequipped to withstand the changes in the weather, because Sørlandet is not only sunhine and summer.

Spornes at the tip of Tromøy

MANY CONSIDER THE SEA BEAUTIFUL WHEN THE STORM RAGES AND THE WAVES SMASH AGAINST THE SHORES. THAT IS BECAUSE THEY DO NOT HAVE TO BE OUT THERE IN THAT WEATHER, BUT CAN RETURN TO THEIR SNUG AND COSY HOMES WHENEVER THEY WANT.

9.9

Contrasts

The fact that the sea is unpredictable and dangerous should not spoil the joys its beauty can offer also in other seasons than summer, because even in freezing temperatures and storm, it is magnificent in Sørlandet.

Understandably, most of us do not wish to live in places where we are dependent on a boat to get to work, or school or day care. Therefore, most of the houses on the islands have become summer places. Those who like using their houses in winter, too, leave their boats out – safely moored – ready to go if necessary or when they feel like it.

On clear, fine winter days the sea is quiet and kind. The fish swim close to the shore in shallow waters. Fresh cod tastes fantastic in a warm room behind windows with lace curtains and ice ferns.

Extreme winter days with temperatures below zero and storm, and cosy summer evenings with tepid water between the rocks – the contrasts are great, nevertheless idyllic each in its own way.

Havsøysund. Same place a freezing winter day and a fine midsummer day.

A stormy autumn day and a fine summer day at Bjellandstrand in Tromøya at Arendal.

The sea is merciless. When the storm rages, the contrast to the summer idyll is huge. There is an enormous distance from the foaming waves bashing relentlessly against the rocks and smashing everything to bits, to the gentle ripples caressing the rocks, one fine summer day. But that is the nature of the coast and we have to learn to live with it.

The older residents would never dream of leaving their boats out unprotected in the more exposed parts of the sea when a storm was brewing. But if you have only experienced the mild face of the sea, it is difficult to imagine that it can change completely almost overnight. But it does, and it can cost – hopefully only materially.

The sea is beautiful. Also when it rises wildly and roars towards land. On such days we have to consider us lucky to have a safe ground underneath our feet and a warm shelter to take refuge in when we have had enough.

In autumn and winter people prefer to be inside. The lights shine through the windows and there are fewer boats on the fjord. But it does not mean that the Southerners are hibernating. Everyday life in Sørlandet is not very different from life in other parts of the country. But as a summer visitor it is easy to get the impression that the Southerners live a laid back life. Undoubtedly, they do know how to enjoy life, and grasp the moments – particularly in summer. But in general, the Southerners are just like everybody else in the country, often stressed and hassled by everyday hustle and bustle.

A winter day at the outer harbour Merdø at Arendal.

A living Sea

The sea currents flow like giant rivers in the sea – some are tremendously powerful, others are weaker. The Atlantic current is the life nerve of our waterways. Without it the temperatures would have been much lower and the sea life would have been different.

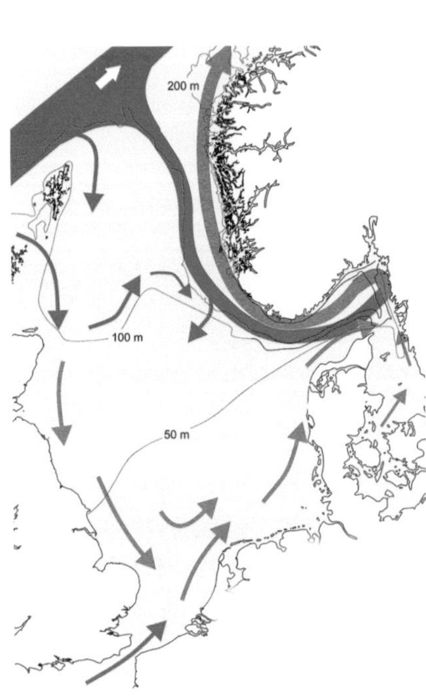

The sea is never still. It is constantly in motion. Even when it looks calm and the surface is like a mirror as far as the eyes can see, there is always movement in the water. Warm water rises and cold water sinks. Saltwater sinks because it is heavier than freshwater, which in turn rises because it is lighter than saltwater.

The coast of Norway is highly affected by the great masses of warm and salty water, the so-called Atlantic water – an extension of the Gulf Stream. Most of this water comes to our coasts through the Faeroe and Shetland canals, and through the Norwegian trench, between Shetland and Norway. The heat from the water gives us a much milder winter climate along the coast than we would have had normally.

One branch of the Atlantic water turns towards Skagerrak because of the earth rotation, and constitutes approximately 80% of the water volume that runs through Skagerrak annually. The rest comes from the North Sea, the coast of Jutland in Denmark and the Baltic sea via Kattegat.

The Norwegian Coastal Current begins in the East of Skagerrak. This current follows the coast to the west and further on to the north of Norway, like a huge layered river. This 'river' brings in on average one million cubic meters of water per second out of Skagerrak. By the time it reaches the west coast, it has becomes gradually more powerful, partly due to the surge of fresh water from the Norwegian rivers, but mainly it blends with the Atlantic water that runs northwards on the outside. Thus, the effects of the Jutland stream and the Baltic Sea are marginalised in the western part. Because of the rotation of the earth the coastal stream stays towards the Norwegian coast, but powerful off-shore winds can press the top layer away from the coast from time to time.

In the last decades, we have seen significant rises in the sea temperature. The deepwater in the North Sea and Skagerrak has had abnormally high winter temperatures. Some are convinced that these are signs of global warming. Others are not as bombastic. They believe that what we are experiencing are only natural variations.

The plankton that floats rather passively in the waters is also an important prerequisite for a living sea. The planktons consist of plant plankton (microscopic algae), animal plankton, jellyfish and bacteria.

The primary production – the growth of plant planktons – is far more vigorous along the coast than further out in the open sea. Primary production also takes place at the bottom by the bentic sea plants, such as kelp forest and the eelgrass meadows. It swarms with life among the sea plants, and in such places thrive juvenile and bigger fishes, lobsters and crabs.

The coastal current transports eggs, larvae, juvenile fish and other marine animals, but also waste and pollution. Consequently, both natural organisms and environmentally harmful substances are spread over large areas of the coast. Fortunately, we have become much better at taking care of the environment, these last years. There is therefore considerably less debris and oil along the coasts than earlier.

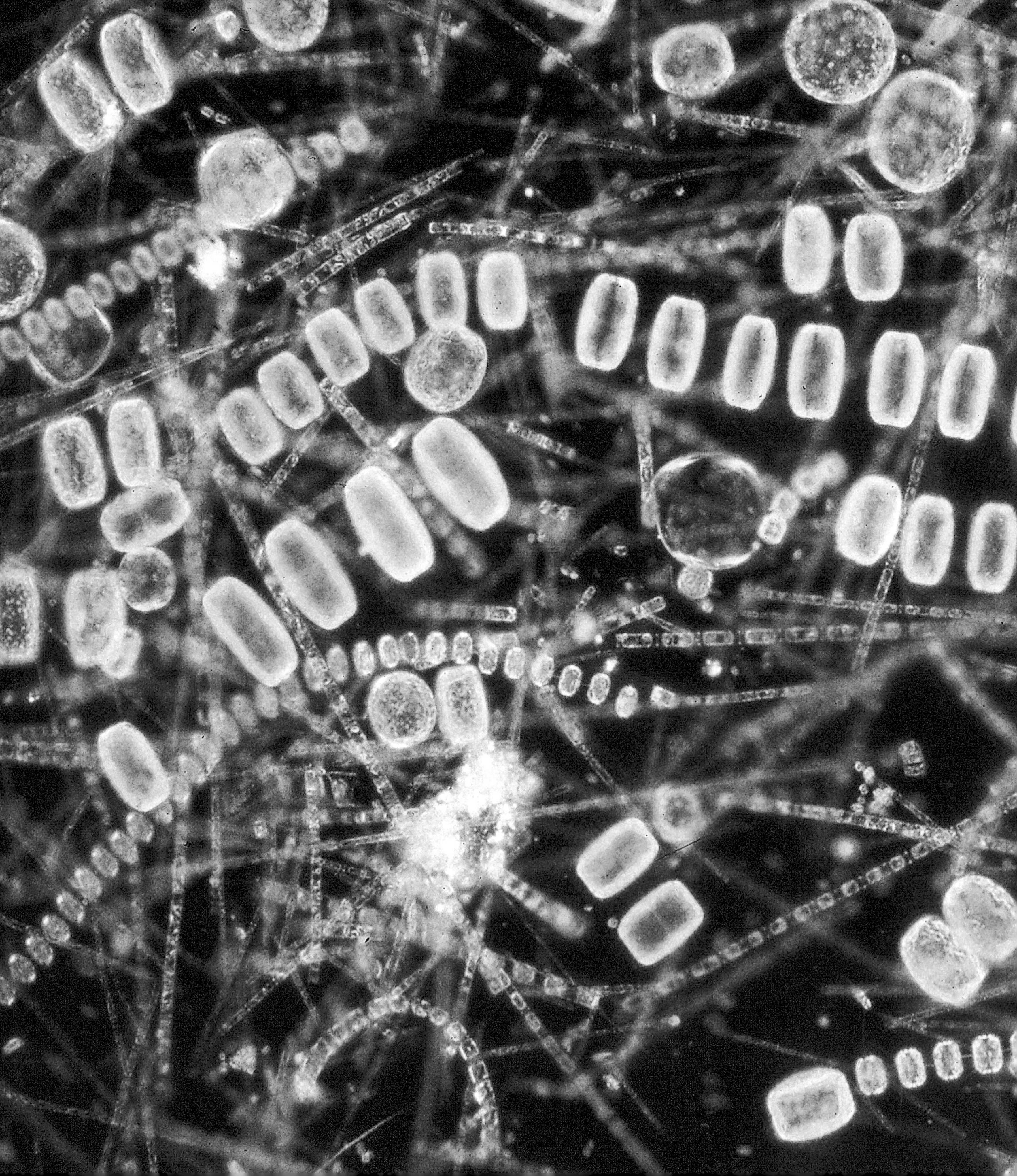

Algae - the Essence of Life in the Sea

The plankton algae are the 'grass of the sea.' A little simplified we can say that the microscopic algae are the essence of life in sea – from shell and crawfish to fish, seal and whales.

By photosynthesis, marine plankton algae convert light energy into chemical energy. Like all other plants they produce chemical compounds (sugar) with carbon dioxide, water and nutrients as raw material and sunlight as energy.

There are more than 4000 different species of marine plankton algae registered. Most of them are good sources of food for animals higher up in the food chain, such as copepods, fish larvae, snails and mussels. However, we also have identified a few dozen plankton algae that produce toxins.

In Skagerrak, the best known is *Chrysochromulina polylepis,* which in May 1988 became extremely poisonous. The effect on the marine fauna along the coast was dramatic. Pictures of dead shell, starfish, ballan wrasse, sea trout and farmed fish, filled the newspapers. The media focus was enormous, with articles and photographs in the biggest magazines, papers and on TV-stations in the country. Also the prestigious magazine, Newsweek, had a large cover story about the *Chrysochromulina* invasion in Southern Norway.

It was a "silent" spring – a spring many of us still remember. The terns flew restlessly about without finding food. The ballan wrasse was gone – it did not bite that year. Many were despaired. Even though the marine fauna and flora was affected, the nature is largely in balance again. Although many fish died, several others sought safety in the depths of the sea, while some, like the eel and the sea trout, escaped to the freshwaters. Nevertheless, most people were jolted by the serious reminder of the fragility of the nature around us. Environmental consciousness was awakened in many people that spring. Even though poisonous algae often come into focus, the 'non-poisonous' plankton algae are as exciting to know. The diversity of plankton algae in sea water varies both with the seasons and with the biological habitats.

In one drop of seawater there are is an incredible variation of plankton algae both regarding form and colour. In some species the cells are connected in long chains, while others live as single cells. Some can move a little with help of their flagella. Whereas others is immobile. The colour of the pigments that gather light can also vary from verdigris green, for example in *Tetraselmis,* to brown and reddish pigments in the dinoflagella, such as *Dinophysis.* When a fresh drop of seawater is studied under the microscope, the colours are fresh and intense. They are simply gorgeous. The intense green colour in some of the plankton algae, and the red colour of some animal plankton will knock out any colour chart.

Each year, during spring, large amounts of plankton algae blossom in the sea along our coast. Great concentration of algae can colour the sea.
It is fantastic to think that plants both under the water and on land use carbon dioxide in the process we call photosynthesis and which is the essence of all life on earth.
While at the same time, the plants produce life giving oxygen.

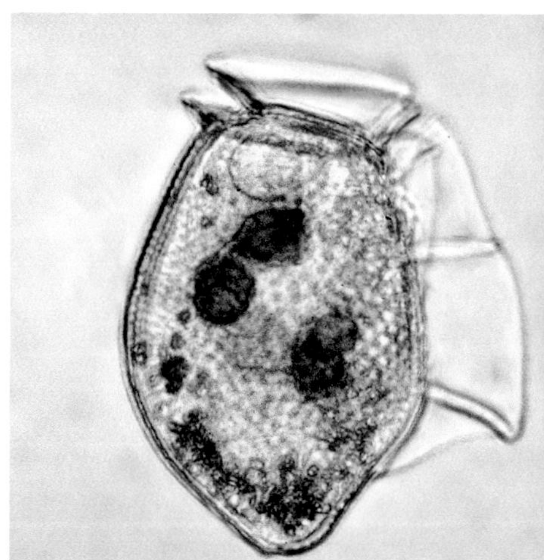

The algae *Dinophysis*, which turns blue mussels poisonous, colours the water red when it appears in high concentrations.

The algae *Thalassiosira*, seen through the microscope in a 200 times magnification.

Broad-nosed pipefish

Life in the Ebb-tide

"With Webbed Feet"

People in Sørlandet are fond of saying that they are born with 'webbed feet.' It is doubtful if they would have said that had they known about all the creatures that live just off the beach. But nothing there is dangerous. Nonetheless, it a little strange and unpleasant to notice suddenly that the beach shrimps are nibbling at your toes. For at the bottom of the sea – between stones, pebbles and seaweed – a multitude of creatures creep and swim. Animals such as sand fleas, shore crabs, starfish, snails and tiny crawfish – not to mention all the juvenile fish.

THE SOUTHERNERS ARE ALLEGEDLY BORN WITH 'WEBBED FEET,' BUT PERHAPS THEY WOULD HAVE PREFERRED TO HAVE THEIR TOES OUT OF THE WATER IF THEY KNEW ABOOUT EVERYTHING THAT MOVES BENEATH THE SURFACE.

In the Low Tide Zone

Day in and day out – all year round – the sea level rises and sinks at specific times of the day. Twice a day the sea level rises creating a high tide, or flow as it is also called, and twice a day it pulls back and we have low tide, or ebb. These high and low tides recur every six hours. In other words, there is a twelve hour interval between each ebb and flow. Since this does not take place at the same time everyday throughout the year, the ebb and flow schedules are announced in the newspapers daily.

Shellfish depend on humid habitat. Even though snails and mussels have the ability to encapsulate themselves they cannot survive many hours without water. They have therefore adapted themselves to the rhythms of the ebb and tide.

The area between the tide mark and the ebb mark is called the littoral, or the low tide zone. In this natural environment, which shifts between dry and wet, live many different sorts of sea plants and animals.

The wart barnacle is a small shellfish that lives inside a calcareous shell. You have certainly seen the white shells sticking to the stones right at the edge of the sea. That is wart barnacle. Many of us have unpleasant experiences with this species, because of their razor sharp edges that cut through our bare feet.

When the wart barnacle is under water its shell opens and the creature fans the water with a feather looking wing. These are feet with long hair with which the wart barnacle pushes water into its shell taking in food and fresh water. During low tide the shell closes to avoid drying out.

One wonders how this creature can reproduce, 'glued' as it is to its foundation. Apparently, there is no need to worry, because the wart barnacle is a particularly well equipped creature concerning this matter. Many of its neighbours are conveniently close to its genitals. In addition, each creature has both the female and male genitals – to be on the safe side!

The wart barnacle is tiny shellfish in a calcareous shell.

The Sandy Beaches

Although the sandy beaches look the same all the time, that is certainly not the case. It just looks like, because wind and sea, ebb and tide constantly move the tiny grains. In between all these grains of sand, live a myriad of countless small animals and plants. Therefore, you often find a multitude of small fish, shells and snails on the sandy bottom just off the shore. These creatures are themselves food for sea-birds and larger fish. When evening approaches, some of the bigger fish swim into the shallow waters in search of food. First in the queue one usually finds the sea trout and the cod.

When walking and wading through the fantastic tepid water lapping the sandy beach, it is almost impossible to imagine that this is a tough habitat for the natural inhabitants of these sandy shores. At other times of the year, they have to cope with highly variable environmental conditions. Therefore, all the species that are not capable of swimming in and out with the ebb and tide are particularly adaptable. They tolerate nearly everything – from broiling heat (30° C) – to bitter cold with many degrees below zero during the winter ebb tide. They have to live with rain and snow and tolerate both saltwater and freshwater, dehydration during low tide, and the constant danger of becoming someone's meal. Undoubtedly, the residents of these sandy shores have a tough life.

The lug worm leaves clear traces in the low tide mark on the sandy beaches, but we seldom see it. It lives in U-shaped burrows in the sandy muddy beds. There it lives like the earthworm, ingesting sand and digesting the organic matters that exit between the grains. When the lug worm is full of sand, it pushes out a long, thin sand sausage in a way that it coils up like sand spaghetti at the bottom of the sea.

Sometimes the lug worm and other polychaetes appear swimming freely in the waters. This happens when they swarm in order to breed. The fish know when to strike. Flounders, cods and sea trout can be full of worms after having dined in shallow sandy water.

That is why, the lug worms are perfect as bait – used in the same way as earthworms. In our neighbouring country in the south, lug worms are valued bait for sea fishing, but in Norway very few people make use of this highly effective bait.
In order to get hold of the worms you have to dig in the sand where you see piles of sand spaghetti – the beach worms' pooh!

The sandy shores are more welcoming beaches. They are the habitat of birds, shells, snails, lug worms, fish and many other sea creatures.

Lug worm

and Lug worm castings

Shellfish on the Menu

Only a few years ago, blue mussels, oyster and cockles were considered as exotic food. But after Norwegians began travelling to the Mediterranean countries, and they experienced the delights of shellfish, many have started using a variety of fresh shellfish. The market for shellfish is now growing fast.

Blue Mussels growing at the bottom of the rocks are the best. In Sørlandet, they grow quickly and can reach market size (approx. 5 cm) within a year. The finest blue mussels are often found where freshwater runs into seawater. The blue mussels filter enormous amounts of water effectively, in search of plankton algae or other sources of food. In fact they are such effective water filters that in some places they are deliberately put out in the sea as a way of improving the quality of the fjord waters. This means that they clean the water for particles and food surplus.

Cockles are found in shallow waters along the whole coast. The cockles – which lie buried in the sand – have two tubes or canals, resembling eyes sticking into the water. With one tube they suck in the water and filter the digestible plankton algae and from the other they pump out water and excrement. The density of cockles in good habitats can be fantastically high, but if the winter is extra harsh, much of the stock can die. The Eurasian oystercatchers can also have a huge impact on the numbers of the stock.

If you wish to eat cockles, the sand must be emptied by hanging them in a net in free water masses for a day or two before they are ready to use.

Blue mussel

Sometimes shells can be poisonous
The reason is that they live by filtering small plankton algae from the seawater. Most of the plankton algae are good sources of nourishment for the shells, but once in a while, the poisonous plankton algae appear in a more concentrated amounts. Then the shells become poisonous, and are inedible for us.

The poisonous plankton algae are neither large nor frightening to look at. The diarrhoea poisons normally come from a group of algae called dinoflagella, the family *Dinophysis* is often the problem. Sometimes, the *Alexcandrium* appear in the waters. Then everyone should avoid shells because they may contain dangerous nerve poisons.

Poisonous shellfish?
When the shellfish have accumulated too much algae poison they become inedible.

Check Norwegian Food Safety Authority's shellfishl warning on Tel: 820 33 33, or on the Internet, or text TV before picking blue mussels. Or buy them from the shop.

Cockles

European Flat Oyster

Oysters should preferably be served raw with lemon and Champagne. But steamed shells can also be good.

European flat oysters(*Ostrea edulis*) enjoy sea water with good 'bathing temperatures,' such as we have had these last few years in Sørlandet. The oysters have now settled in the outer end of the Skagerrak coast. It is relatively easy to get hold of some oysters, because they are spread over such vast areas. Earlier, oysters were mostly found in enclosed bays deep inside the archipelago, where only those who had local knowledge knew where to find them.

The oysters spawn in warm water, and the high summer temperatures in 1994, 1997 and 2002, are probably the reason why we now find more oysters than earlier. During these summers, the water temperature along the whole coast climbed to about 22°C – high enough to allow the oysters to spawn.

Many of us who travel along the coast have found old oyster shells in sandy bays and beaches. We can only guess where these old shells come from. We have to go back to the 1950s to find such high temperatures during summer as we have today. Maybe they are shells from that period spread along the beaches? Oysters can become old – almost 30 years, meaning that they can lie there waiting for the optimal conditions to reproduce.

European Flat Oysters are found inbetween one to five meters deep water and can be easily fetched with a simple diving mask. Generally oysters consume less poisonous algae than blue mussels do. So when the blue mussels are safe to eat, you can be sure that the oysters are too.

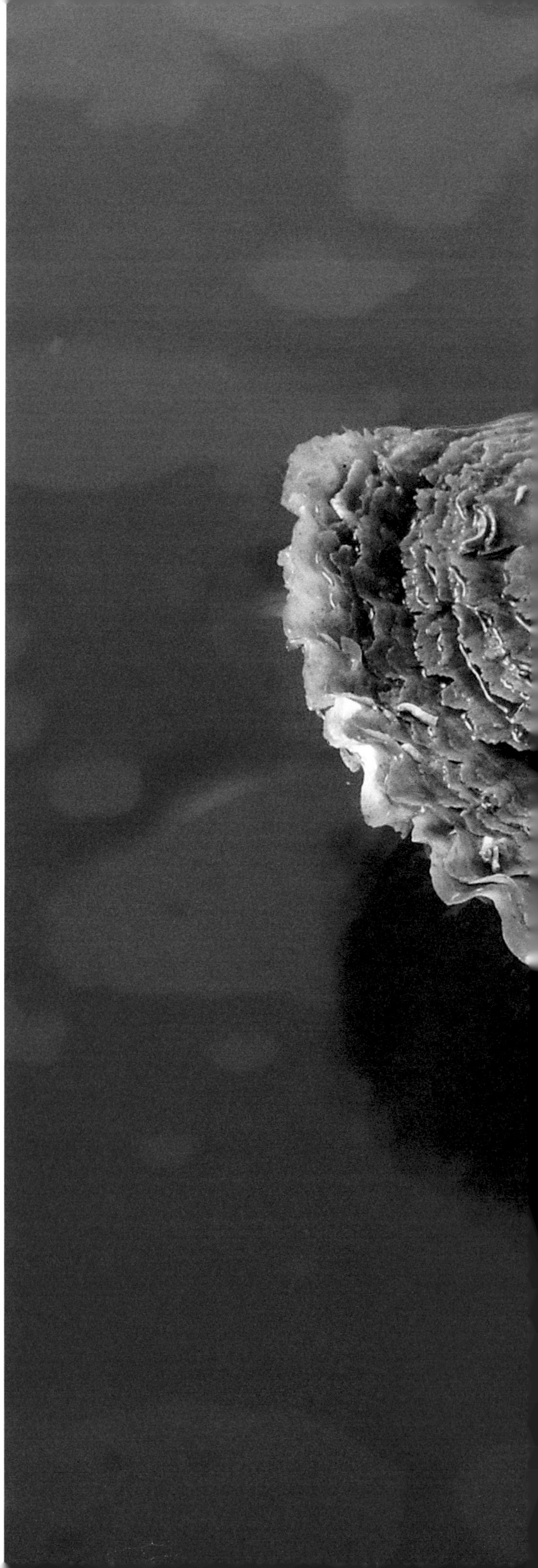

Oysters

Snails - Bait and Delicacy

Many have used coastal snail as bait. But to gather snails for food is unfamiliar for most Norwegians. Both periwinkles and common whelk are edible. They do not absorb algae poisons as mussels do, and they are usually delicious and safe to eat.

Periwinkles or the coastal snails are very common and there are several species. The characteristic rounded forms are easy to recognize. The snails are highly valued natural baits – especially for ballan wrasse fishing with float. If you fill the hook with one or a couple of smashed snails to hide it, you get a super bait. This bait is also very effective for cod fishing in the kelp forest.

French people visiting Norway are surprised at the number of snails we have on our shores, and their size. In France, snails are popular food and are served in every restaurant with respect for itself. In the past few years, there has been some export of coastal snails from Sørlandet to France, which is just as well since so few Norwegians appreciate this 'French' delicacy.

The Common whelk has white delicate meat which looks more tempting than the beach snail's. Most people who taste common whelk, find it very tasty. The muscular foot though needs extra care. It should be cooked about half an hour to acquire that exquisite tenderness. It can then be seasoned and baked.

You cannot pick common whelks in the low tide zone. But you can get them as a bonus catch when fishing crabs in traps in deep water.

Netted dog whelks are peculiar creatures. They usually live in shallow water with sandy and muddy bottom, and are easily recognizable by the characteristic lattice structure on their shells. Netted dog whelks are scavengers and predators, but can also digest the organic matter in the sediment. The snails have a phenomenal sense of smell. Throw a mussel or a fish head in the water, and it does not take many minutes before the snails begin flocking around the "food."

The purple snail was highly affected by the 1988 algae catastrophe. Today, the purple snail has recovered and is again a common sight on the tip of the shores on the islets farthest out into the sea.

The common limpet is is difficult to detach when it is stuck to the rock. But at night, the snails begin to wander about and ingest the nutritious matters existing in the rocks. Did you know that the common limpet has been used to soothe sore nipples for over 1000 years in Norway? The smooth mother-of-pearl inside surface of the shell is supposed to have a soothing effect, but the snail has to be cooked and cleaned before use.

Common limpet

Purple snail

Periwinkle or coastal snail

Netted dog whelk

Common whelk

Common Shore Crab

Shore crabs are undervalued as food. In fact, they have a fantastic taste and perfectly suitable for making fish or shellfish soup. The good taste is due to large amounts of free amino acids in the animal's tissue. This is the same stuff that is found in both common crabs and lobsters, but shore crabs have definitely the most – hence the good taste.

Shore crab as bait is an effective weapon when bottom fishing for cod. The same amino acids giving the fantastic taste to the shellfish soup also attract the fish.
In this connection, we would like to promote the bait bag. In the old days, fishermen never went off line fishing without their bait bags.
Old line fishers had their own crab traps down at the bottom. Shore crabs were smashed in a mortar and stuffed in the bait bag, which was then hoisted down into the sea to attract the fish. Moreover, it was important that the boats were moored together, side by side. Not only for the sake of socializing, but because they all got more fish if they stuck together. Several bait bags attracted more fish than a single one.

Shore crabs are robust animals and can be kept in a bucket of water and let out again. It is great fun for the children who love to fish shore crabs. The crabs bob up and down in the seawater, which in the bucket can quickly rise above 20°C on a warm summer day. It is therefore a good thing that the shore crab is so sturdy.

Is there anything more pleasant than fishing shore crabs with the children on a day off in summer?
All you need is a clothespin and some string, a bit of smashed mussel and a touch of patience.
The catch can be cooked in the kitchen and used as a taste enhancer for the holidays' most delicious fish or shellfish soup.

Put the shore crabs in boiling seawater for a couple of minutes.
Clean the crabs by cracking the shells and removing the internal organs, as you do when cleaning a common crab.
Sautee the crushed crabs in oil heated in a pan.
Pour a little water and let it poach for 15 minutes.
Transfer it to a sieve and use the stock in a fish soup with vegetables, tinned tomatoes, mussels, ballan wrasse, cod, shrimps and other fresh seafood you have at hand.

Shore crab

The Jellyfish

Sometimes there are many jellyfish in the sea. At other times there are almost none. What is the reason?

Unfortunately the jellyfish often appears as soon as the seawater reaches suitable temperature for a bath. Along the Southern Coast the sea temperature rises following a few days with breeze from the south. The sea breeze also brings along stinging jellyfish, pushing them together in great numbers inside the archipelago. However, this usually happens after a few days with offshore wind, which draws up the stinging jellyfish from the deeper water. Sometimes it is impossible to swim without getting stung.

But if the seawater rises up to 20°C, the stinging jellyfish which prefers colder water retreats to deeper waters again.

In contrast to the stinging jellyfish, moon jellyfish tolerate warm water well. Jellyfish not only look like jelly, they are jelly! They belong to a group of animals called jelly plankton because they contain a lot of water and have a body that both looks and feels like jelly. Jellyfish contain nearly a hundred percent water. Nevertheless, they are very effective predators. Posion is their assault weapon. When the jellyfish wants to eat, it stuns its prey with the poison inside its tentacles and then swallows it. Fish eggs and plankton are its main prey.

The jellyfish has stinging cells with poison that numbs and kills the prey. Nearly all jellyfish have stinging tentacles. In the common jellyfish the poison is so weak that we humans do not react to it when we get it on our hands or feet. But try to lick your fingers after you have lifted a jellyfish and you will discover a stinging sensation on your tongue.

The moon jellyfish looks like a transparent 'flying saucer.' When eating, it fans the food in with the small threads that are densely packed along the edges. In this way, the food is directed into the mouth located in the middle under the jellyfish. If you hold a moon jellyfish up against the sun, you can see the canal systems, the mouth and the stomach.

Stinging jellyfish have both long and short stinging tentacles. The largest stinging jellyfish can have threads that stretch out about 20 meters behind that orangey lump of jelly. Good to keep in mind when swimming among jellyfish.

Blue jellyfish can resemble a common jellyfish with long tentacles. However, it is a stinging jellyfish that has as poisonous tentacles as the orange stinging jellyfish.

In addition, there are small jellyfish that resemble translucent gooseberries and gherkins. They do not have nettle cells and are completely harmless for humans and fish. For some types of fish, for example the lumpfish, it is a delicacy.

Moon jellyfish

Stinging jellyfish

Beautiful, Poisonous and Tasty

The colours on the greater weever's head are beautiful, with their blue, green and light brown hues. It is rather surprising that this attractive fish can be so poisonous. But it is a little unpleasant as it lies hidden in the sand with its malignant poisonous spikes sticking out – thankfully, most of the time out of reach from small children's feet.

Most people know about the greater weever, because it is the most poisonous and dangerous fish along the Southern Coast. On fine summer days, the greater weever has a nasty tendency to lie buried right off the sandy beaches, at depth up to a couple of meters. Therefore, it is good to know that the greater weever seldom digs itself down in shallower water. But it happens, and then you can have the bad luck to get stung by its poisonous glands.

"Like a viper's bite," say those who have experienced the poisonous glands and can tell about excruciating immediate pain. Nervously, they tell the stories about the fisherman who ended up with stiff fingers for the rest of his life. Others who have been bitten talk about some immediate pain after being bitten, passing nausea, but the symptoms are fleeting.

The general advice, nowadays, is to visit a doctor if one is bitten. This is particularly important with children. The poison that is pressed out of the spikes and into the wound usually induces quite strong pains. Sometimes it can also cause swelling and redness around the punctured skin. The best treatment is warm water until you get to a doctor. Just put the foot or arm in ca. 40°C warm water for half an hour or more. It usually becomes better after that. It is advisable to take an allergy tablet if there is a danger for allergic reactions.

Although many people have been bitten without any permanent injury, undoubtedly we have to respect the greater weever.

The greater weever arrives when the sea temperature rises – for it is only when the water temperature is good for swimming that the greater weever enters the scene. It swims in its characteristic manner, with breast fins straight out and tail slightly waddling. Nevertheless, it swims with dignity and other fish retreat as the greater weever approaches majestically moving in the water. Perhaps they, too, fear its poisonous glands?
During the night the greater weever sets out in search of food, which consists of small fish and various shellfish such as shrimps and other amphipods.

Greater weever is a tasty fish, which we have learnt to appreciate because of our Danish friends. When preparing it, cut away the whole head and the uppermost part of the back, so as to be sure to avoid the poison glands. The back fins upfront and both gills are poisonous. The tail, however, has fine, light and succulent meat.

Fishing in July

Holiday fishing

In July most Norwegians take their summer holiday. We head off to the coast – either to live in a tent, a cottage, or on a boat. Many people also dream of big time fishing

But when the sun is broiling hot and the water is warm, it is not so easy to find fish that will take the bait. Nevertheless, it is not impossible to catch fish in summer. You just have to do some alternative fishing.

Fishing in deep water using natural bait will give results, even on warm summer days.

IS HARD TO LURE THE FISH TO TAKE THE BAIT

Natural Bait gives more Fish

Mackerels often like speed and it may be a good idea to vary your speed when trolling.

When the water temperature rises to 17-20 degrees Celsius, most large fish leave the usual fishing places close to shore for lower temperatures in deeper water. Therefore, the number one advice to hobby fishers is to fish in deeper water. That means you should find a place between 25 and 50 meters deep if you want large cod, coalfish and pollock. If you are happy with whiting and small cod, you can try closer to shore, but avoid fishing in the middle of the day. Go early in the morning or just before sundown.

In summer, it is often a good idea to fish with natural bait. Fish that are unwilling to take spinning bait usually cannot resist fresh baits. When fishing with bottom lines, raw shrimps or fresh mussels are perfect to use on the hook. But the most important thing is to know the best fishing spots. Therefore, use some time to get to know the area. Study the sea map, talk to the locals and experiment. In the old days, the fishermen kept the good fishing spots to themselves. Nowadays, they are more forthcoming and the majority are happy to give you some good tips.

The mackerel usually arrives after a few days with 'easterly wind' and strong onshore currents. Then you have to be ready with your boat and fishing lines. There have been fair numbers of mackerel the past few years, all the way along the Skagerrak coast in the middle of summer.

The mackerel is best to eat early in the season. Some people find it too fatty later in the summer, while others enjoy its delicious taste throughout the season. The good thing with mackerel is that it can be prepared in many ways: fried, poached, smoked or pickled. In Sørlandet, it is generally eaten freshly fried with cold rhubarb soup for dessert.

The mackerel is normally easiest to catch in the mornings and in the evenings. If you do not catch anything with the usual lines that you can get in sport fishing shops, you should try replacing the shiny hooks or rubber worms with simple black hooks size 4 or 5. It actually seems like the mackerel prefers these.

The garpike follows the mackerel, and if you are an eager mackerel fisher you have probably noticed that the garpike arrives to the coast a little before the mackerel. When you have one on the hook, it feels like as if you have a mackerel, for garpike 'drives' the fishing line from side to side in the same manner as the mackerel does. But when you bring the fish close to the boat, you can suddenly hear the 'unmistakable 'whisking' sound with the characteristic mouth on the surface of the water. Then you know that it is a 'miss,' because the garpike is not particularly good to eat, and is difficult to get off the hook, being so slippery. When you are finished, your hands stinks all day no matter how much you wash them.

The children, on the other hand think it is a cool fish and call it swordfish.

You can catch flatfish with the bait at the bottom. One fish that tolerates warm water is the turbot. This flatfish keeps to the sand banks in shallow waters during summer, where it spawns between May and August.

The turbot is an exquisite food. The Romans called it the "pheasant of the sea." The whiting is called "the chicken of the sea," and the difference between the two in taste and availability is well illustrated by their names, because the turbot is not an easy fish to catch with bait and hook. If you want turbot, your best chances are with fishnets or long lines along the bottom of the sea. But it is important to use bait that moves lightly and loosely over the sand bank, easy to see. Analysis of the stomach contents have shown that the turbot's preferred food is small fish swimming in schools over the sandy bottom.

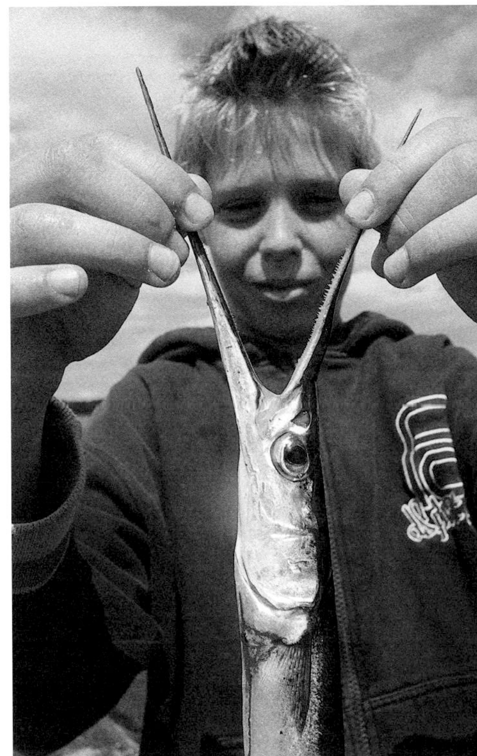

Garpike

Fly-fishing in the Low Tide

In large parts of the Skagerrak coast the sea trout stock is good, and you find this delicious fish along the whole coast, both in the fjords and between isles and rocks in the outer end of the archipelago.

Eager fly fishers have discovered that the population of sea trout is fairly good, and often you can see people at dusk in wading trousers elegantly swinging their fly lines.

The sea trout is called the Queen of the seas and it is much more exotic and difficult to catch than mackerel and coalfish.

Try fishing in between islets and rocks, preferably in places with currents. The best time to fish is at dawn and dusk because then the sea trout seeks shallow water in search of food. Stomach content analyses show that large sea trout prefer herrings, sprat and sometimes sand eels. Therefore, the best spinning parts are those who resemble these fishes, and the lure should move fast by fits and starts.

Fly fishing in late winter is fun, often with good catch. Cod and coalfish bite the flies willingly, even though the sea trout is the main target for most fly fishers. Catching sea trout is not limited to spring and summer, although the 'textbooks' claim that the sea trout sets out up the river to spawn and does not return to the sea before the following spring. But as we know, theory and practice do not always correspond.

Freshwater trout and saltwater trout are the same species. Some of them choose to migrate to the sea and are called sea trout. Considering the poor conditions under which they live in the small streams, it is not surprising that they choose to swim out to the sea where their access to food is far better. We do know that spawning sea trouts are in the streams for just a few weeks before they move back to the sea.

The areas with brackish water are the sea trout's domain during winter. There it finds food in the muddy banks. Since the sea trout is originally a freshwater fish, the smallest fish have problems with the salt balance as the temperature sinks in the sea during winter. The larger fish do not have the same problem with the salt balance as the small fish do, and tolerate the transition between freshwater and saltwater better. It seems that the availability of food determines the big fish dwelling place. The large sea trout are often found in the middle of the fjord in search of herrings. But during dusk they often seek food in shallow areas.

The sea trout eats whatever is easily available at the time. We know that the juvenile sea trout, which weighs about 300-500 grams, and in winter stays in the shallow parts of the fjord, has a different diet from the large trout in the deep. The smallest trout feed on a wide spectre of animals such as polychaetes (sand worms), amphipods, isopods and shrimps, and small fishes like sand gobies and two-spotted gobies. The large sea trout – from 750 grams upwards – seems to prefer herring and sprat, which can be found both in the fjords and all the way out towards the coast.

Only Small Cod to Get?

"You can only get small cods!" the South Coast fishermen have been reporting, these last few years. It has not been totally unexpected, because the West Coast of Sweden has been in a similar situation for some time. In Norway, the first reports came from the East Coast and now from the Southern Coast. What is happenning exactly?

In recent years, researchers at the Institute of Marine Research have studied the cod stocks from Hvaler to Lillesand, and the results are both exciting and interesting.

The results from the last few years compared to similar studies, done in 1985–89, seem to indicate that there are actually more cods in Arendal and Lillesand now than before. But the large cods are missing. When it comes to the situation around the Oslo fjord from Hvaler and Vasser and part of the Kragerø Archipelago, the studies show that there are far fewer cods than earlier. In these areas, only small cods are available. Bigger cods are completely non-existent. In Kragerø, the cod stock was better than in the outer part of the Oslo fjord, but not anywhere as good as the stock in the Southern Coast.

It is difficult to point out specific reasons for the decrease in the coastal cod stocks. Recent research show that there seems to be enough spawning cods to sustain a strong annual stock. But during summer much of the juvenile fish die. The juvenile fish obviously lose in the competition for food and shelter during growth. Small cods are bonus catch in intensive eel fishing with traps,, and increased stocks of cormorants and seals, particularly in the eastern parts can also be important reasons for the decrease.

The increasing number of summer guests and sport fishers may also have considerable effect on the size of the stock. In addition, there is rigorous fishing activity even in the spawning areas in the fjord.

There is little doubt, however, that fewer cod larvae drift in from the main stock in the North Sea, because the numbers in that stock are at critical level. Whether the cod inhabiting the feeding grounds along the Skagerrak Coast stem from the local stocks along the coast or from the main cod stock in the North Sea, is among the questions the researchers are concerned with most. They have taken genetic samples from juvenile and adult cod throughout the Skagerrak coast in order to answer this question, and are naturally anxious to see the results.

Juvenile cod

Where Does the Cod Swim?

The cods in coastal areas are place bound fish. Studies performed in the Southern Coast shows that the majority of the coastal cods swim only a few hundred meters from where they were let out. The cods' favourite habitat though varies with the size of the fish. The smallest fish, or the 0-group, as we call it, are normally found in the areas near the spawning spots inside the fjord – especially in places with eelgrass meadows. Here, we can find several hundred small cods in an area about 200-300 m^2. The larger cods prefer the deeper areas and love the kelp forests off coast. Most cods between 20 and 40 cm live in the kelp forests, at a depth of 7 to 20 meters, at the outer end of the archipelago. Here, you also find the biggest cods. When it is seven to ten degrees in one meter deep water, the chances are good for catching large cod in such areas.

Many people wonder why the kelp forests and the eelgrass are such important habitats for the fish. The main reason is quite simply that in these areas the fish find plenty of food and good shelters. Among the eelgrass and kelp forests there are endless numbers of shelters and protected areas for both plants and animals. The production in such areas is much higher than in areas where the seabed is covered with ordinary pebbles or mud. The kelp forest and eelgrass meadows house so many species that they can be called underwater 'rain forests.' Here there are a number of animals such as isopods and amphipods, polychaetes, snails, mussels, lobsters, moss animals and fungi, and all the fishes of course.

Everyone who is interested in sea fishing wonders where in this waters surrounding of the archipelago the cod lives. Where are the best fishing spots?

In early spring, you can get a lot of cod in the muddy areas where the fish 'feast' on polychaetes (sand worms). This is perhaps the easiest time to catch cod.

Tagged cod
By marking cods, the researchers can find out how far the fish move and how fast they grow. They can also acquire statistics on how much fish sport fishers catch compared to professional fishers. The cod is usually marked right under the back fin with so-called Floytags. Each cod has its own number, and often there is a prize for anyone who finds one.

European Pollock and Coalfish

The most characteristic feature about the pollock, which is from the cod family, is probably its protrusion. One can easily detect that the lower jaw is slightly over the upper jaw. In addition it has an arched side line. The pollock can become more than one meter long and weigh about 10 kg.

The fish connoisseurs and gourmets become blissful the moment they hear the name pollock. It is probably the firm consistency and the mild taste they are all addicted to, but to be honest it is a wonderful feeling to get a pollock on the hook!

The pollock is an exciting sport fish. A look at the powerful muscles along the back fin reveals its strength. A large pollock tugs like a salmon the moment it is on the hook. But in contrast to the noble salmon, it is not very resilient. After a couple of minutes fight, it becomes quiet at the end of the line – suspiciously quiet. As a result, the fisher usually relaxes and eagerly begins to pull the fish in on land. At that moment, the pollock jerks the line and disappears into the deep.

The best time for fishing pollock is end of October, beginning of November. In that period, the large fish gather at regular places out at the tip of the archipelago to "feasts on the herrings," as the fishermen say. Later they return to the fjord to deeper water to spawn.

The pollock is often easy to catch before it wanders into the fjord. A herring like lure or a red rubber worm is often very effective.

When diving in the kelp forest, you can recognize the pollock by the distinguished way it calmly swims by but always at a proper distance.

Pollock

The pollock lives mostly at the bottom of the sea but is also seen partly in schools, when the large fish gather to spawn. It is not unusual to see a school of small fish as well that stay in places with strong currents or over kelp forests.

Its main prey is fish, particularly herring and-sand eels, but shrimps, isopods and amphipods are also part of its diet.

Without doubt the pollock stock in the Southern Coast is drastically reduced over the last thirty years. Studies of juvenile pollock done by the Institute of Marine Research have documented a dramatic decline in their abundance. But from time to time, there are still reports of large fish at the bottom of the sea outside the archipelago, at 60 to 80 meters depth.

Coalfish is not as distinguished for sport fishers as the pollock. It can be called the hobby fishers' consolation prize, because coalfish is very easy to bait and perhaps the most usual fish to catch when fishing from land in the archipelago.

Quite undeservedly, the coalfish has acquired the reputation of being a mediocre food. The taste is not as refined, but coalfish is fantastic as a basic ingredient in coalfish patties – preferably with chives picked from the outer edges of the isles and rocks, or baked in the oven with a dash of herbs from your garden.

Coalfish

Fishing from the Rocks

Fishing from the rocks with long poles, floats and natural bait is a fantastic summer activity, because the ballan wrasses, which feed on barnacles and mussels in shallow water, are easy to bait even on the warmest summer days. The ballan wrasses are rebuked, but undeservedly.

Fishing from the rocks engages both children and adults, because the ballan wrasse is a 'fighter.' It tugs and pulls vigorously and you have to use your strength to pull it in. In addition, it is tasty grilled, smoked or as a main ingredient in a fish soup. It has a strong taste with distinct crabby aftertaste.

Ballan wrasse fishing is best on days when there is strong south-westerly wind. When the waves are high and hit the shore in foamy spurts, you have perfect conditions for fishing.

Watch out for slippery rocks. Use a life vest if you are fishing from slippery rocks where it is difficult to get back on land if you fall into the sea.

When you fish with natural bait, you also tempt of course other fish. If you let the bait sink a little deeper, preferably to the bottom, you may catch both cod and flounder.

"The head of the ballan wrasse is the best part of the whole fish and can compete with the finest Christmas cured meat."
Gabriel Scott (from *Blaaskjeld* 1923)

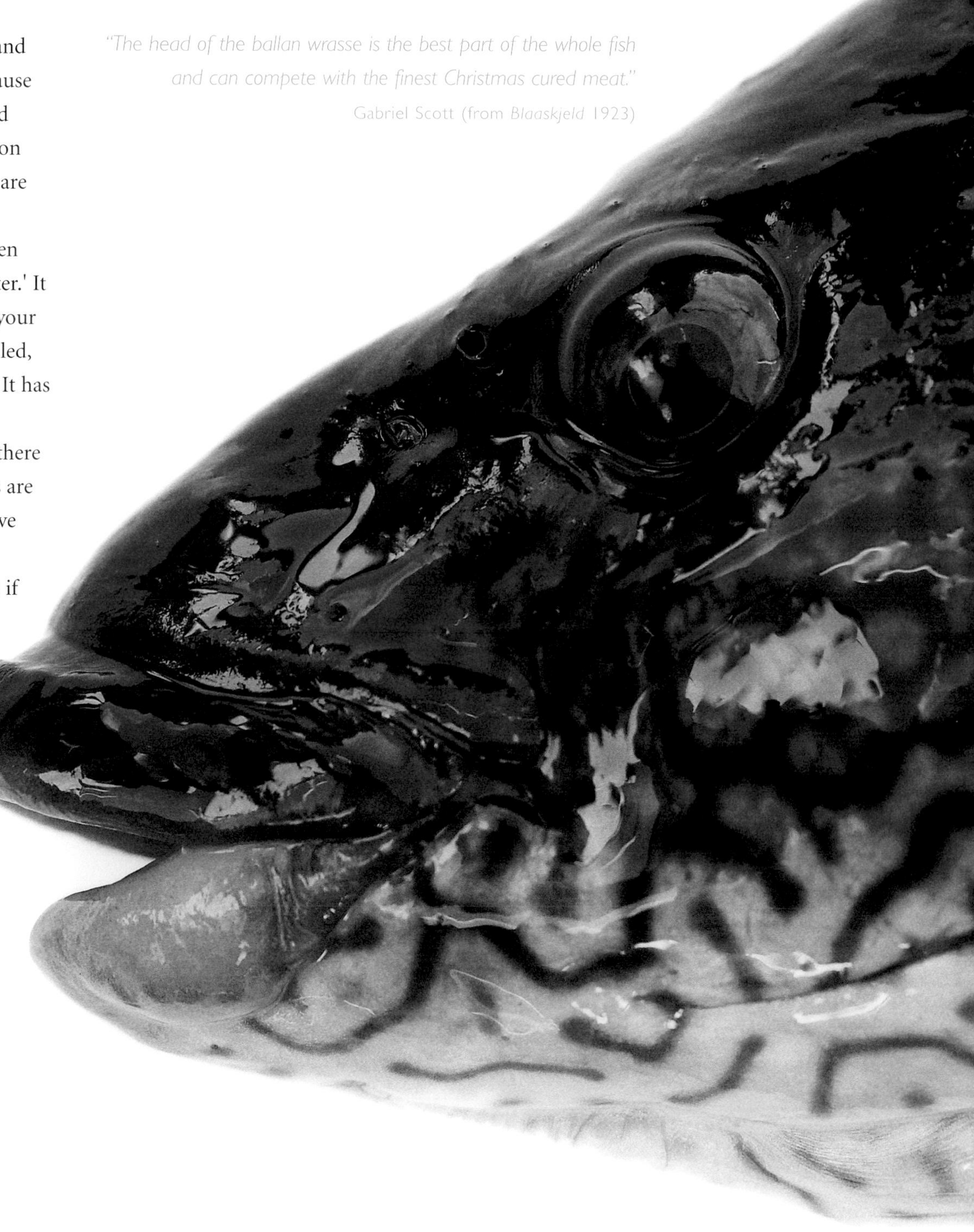

If you want to fish ballan wrasse, you have to go the outermost rocks all the way out into the sea. Use a long telescope pole, preferably an old-fashioned bamboo pole with a float, and nylon lines about 0.40-0.45 mm thick and a little worm hook. As bait use a beach snail without its shell. Then just wait for the big fish.

Do You Know the Wrasse?

If you had told a professional fisherman twenty years ago that the wrasse would become an important source of income, he would have thought you were mad. Today, however, all coastal fishermen know about this fish that has provided a welcome income.

Many people will probably wonder who is willing to pay so much money for a few pathetic shore fish – because it is as shore fish most of us know the wrasse. Who hasn't lain flat as a pancake on the dock with a fishing pole and a little bait on the hook and watched the goldsinny systematically 'clean' the hook, but not swallow the baits.

It is precisely this ability to clean that has turned out to be so useful, because the wrasse do not only clean the bait off the hook. They also clean farmed salmons from parasites. The parasites we are talking about are the salmon lice, which have been a great problem for the fish farming industry for many years. Even though they have been vaccinated, there is still a need for the wrasse as a biological protection against the salmon lice.

There are six species of wrasse in Norway, but only a few of them are used for biological delicing of the farmed salmons. The goldsinny is the most commonly used fish. This has to do primarily with the large number of goldsinny in our waters and its low availability in the North and Western Coast of Norway.

There is an enormous abundance of wrasse in the Southern Coast. Therefore, first class wrasse is imported from the South Coast to the fishing farms in the West Coast.

It is otherwise quite clear that the ballan wrasse is adapted to a diet with much shellfish. They have a kind of "shell crusher" in their throats. It crushes and grinds the shellfish before the stomach takes over. Their teeth are also powerful, and the ballan wrasse can easily bite through the shell of a wart barnacle. If when snorkelling you sneak up to a biggish ballan wrasse feeding on small wart barnacles and mussels, you can clearly hear the "click-click" sound that the wrasse make when they tear loose the shells and wart off the rocks. As you know sound carries well under the water.

The wrasse are warmth loving fish that have reduced activity during the colder seasons. For a long time, we thought that these fish recede to the deep waters to spend the winter there. Lately, however, we have discovered that the labridae do not withdraw to the great depths but swim down to about 15-20 meters deep, where they find places in the cracks and crevices in the mountains for the duration of winter.

In many ways one can say that the labridae hibernates through the winter.

Biological warfare

The fish farming industry saves large sums of money by fighting the salmon lice biologically, using the wrasse to eat the parasites instead of chemicals to get rid of the lice. Undoubtedly, the biological methods are also preferable for the environment around the farming.

Goldsinny eating salmon lice off a farmed salmon

The cuckoo wrasse is colourful – both the male and female form. Few fish in Norwegian waters are more beautiful than the cuckoo wrasse, as it moves carefully among the seaweeds. But the fish sort is colourful in more ways than one. It has a unique life cycle. Well, strictly speaking it is not quite unique. The deep water shrimp also changes its sex. With the cuckoo wrasse 'the whole thing' is rather complicated. Most small cuckoo wrasses are females and look very different, being reddish brown. Some of these though are males with the same female characteristics. These types remain male all their lives. But then something unexpected happens: Some of the females turn into males when they approach six-seven years. The prize for this sexual metamorphosis is that the male becomes the head of a large harem.

When the chief cuckoo wrasse dies, the highest ranking female in the hierarchy takes over. In other words, this is organized according to a social system. Nature can be strangely complicated, seen from our point of view and understanding.

Maintaining the biological diversity is important. But many people find the arguments presented by the environmental authorities incomprehensible and question why an area must be protected when it has no special utility value. One important question is: Can we really know which species and areas will become valuable in the future? Do the areas contain species that the future societies will perhaps find useful?

The wrasse can in this context be a good example. Fifteen years ago, the wrasse had little value in Norway. Today, the situation has changed. Both the environmental authorities and the fish farming community praise this 'cleaning fish' that removes parasites from the farmed fishes and saves the environment from unforeseen side effects of the salmon lice. Unexpected? Absolutely.

The labridae are highly underestimated. The small bait snatchers are worth their weight in gold for the fish farmers, and the larger labridae are tasty food that deserve a better destiny than just being used as baits in lobster pots.

Goldsinny fighting over the bait

Cuckoo wrasse in the kelp forest

'The wife' of the cuckoo wrasse

Crabbing on a Summer Night

You never forget it once you have experienced a light summer night with successful crab fishing. Whether it is the new underwater world we find most fascinating, or the pleasant gathering of friends around the fire while the crabs cook, is actually immaterial.

Summer is the best time of the year to take crabs on the 'edge.' The crabs have the habit of crawling up all the way to the shore on summer nights to eat blue mussels and wart barnacles.

The concentration of crabs are highest out on the outermost isles and rocks. The weather must therefore be fine, and the sea calm, when you set out crabbing in full moon during low tide.

Some years there are great numbers of crabs. You can almost stand on the shore and pick up crabs like mushroom in the woods.

In his book, *Blue mussels*, Gabriel Scott fantasizes about why the crabs crawl up from deep water up on 'land:' "*It crawls out of the water and sits on the barnacle and gazes at the moon – and then the fishermen come and pick it up before it manages to count to three.*"

There is no need for much equipment to pick a pan full of crabs. A powerful torch or a car battery with a floodlight is perfect. In addition, you need a landing net or a rake. Somehow, it is wisely organised that the clock has to approach midnight before the crabs creep properly up towards the shallow waters. While you wait, you have time to find a good place to make a bonfire, eat a little and drink a cup of coffee before the hunt begins.

The crabs should be cooked in saltwater for 15-20 minutes and cooled down on their backs. Many people consider freshly cooked crabs as the ultimate summer food.

When the seawater is nice and warm during midsummer, it can also be exciting to catch crabs by scubadiving. It is easy, all you need is a good underwater torch, a mask and a snorkel. The catch is almost in the pot. This is an event in which children also love to participate. For them it is really exciting to dive into the dark water. They get to see a wildlife that they never have seen before, which is stimulating for their interest in nature. The advantage of diving is that you can reach the crabs that are in deeper places than the low tide zone, and provide a feast in a short time.

Food Foraging or Hobby

From the Sea Larder

The joy of seeing a wriggling live cod come over the edge of the boat is enormous, whether you are a professional fisher or a hobby fisher. Harvesting the resources of the sea never seems to go out of fashion – simply because fresh seafood is too attractive and its taste irresistible.

It is like a deep rooted need for many of us who live on coast, to go out to our sea larder from time to time to fetch fresh food. It feels both right and good to eat fish you have caught yourself.

Some people claim that the majority nowadays cannot be bothered to engage in hobby fishing to supply their own fish. It may be so, but if you ask the boat people who invade the Southern Coast what they've been doing, many of them enthusiastically talk about their hobby fishing. Therefore it is not quite true that hobby fishing has gone out of fashion. It is the most popular hobby in Norway, after photography.

WHAT MAKES PEOPLE SET OUT IN BOATS IN ALL SORTS OF WEATHER
TO CATCH A WRETCHED LOBSTER?

Color Line

The Ownerless Sea

One or two professional fishers may grumble that the hobby fishers are trespassing "their" areas, but in principle it is 'free for all' Norwegian citizens, providing they abide the rules.

Nevertheless, the fishing regulations have some restrictions concerning the use of nets and fishpots for hobby fishers, but most people find these rules both right and fair. For foreign tourists however the quota is 15 kg fish. In addition, there are rules concerning the minimum size of certain types of fish. In Sørlandet it is not allowed to take cod smaller than 30 cm. More info on www.fiskeridir.no.

Earlier on, combination fishing, that is combining fishing with other professions, was rather customary. They were small farmers, teachers, carpenters or sailors. During certain periods of the years, the sea was generous and there they found what they needed.

After a while fishing became more specialized. The technological development opened up for completely new possibilities. In the beginning of the former century (1900), fishing was a profession which became increasingly more common along the whole coast.

After the war and to the present day, many moved away from the islands and small harbours, particularly in the period up to 1970. The pretty south coast houses out in the skerries were sold to summer guests. Even though the authorities tried to counter the resettlement through legislation, many of the islands nowadays only come to life for a few short weeks each summer.

The professional fishers followed the migrants and became 'land crabs.' The children of the fishermen took higher education, because everyone understood that the future society required people with theoretical knowledge.

According to a population count from 1948, there were about 2500 people who had fishing as their main profession along the coast of Skagerrak. In 1971, the number had fallen to about 800 people. In 2006, it is assumed that less than 700 people are professional fishers in the Southern Coast.

There are only a handful of people who still carry on fishing in small boats, the old fashioned way. They change between fishing eels, labridae, crabs in summer, lobster in autumn and cod in autumn and spring. With many hours at sea they are able to earn a normal salary.

The fishers who have managed best are the shrimp trawlers. The incomes are still good because the catch is favourable and the prices high. Moreover, the equipment has become much better in recent years.

All in all, the general impression is that the pressure on our marine resources is much less than before, since the professional fishers have decreased so dramatically in number. We must however not forget that the number of equipments have increased considerably in the last few years. The technological development offers many good solutions: nylon nets, winches, net cleaners, echo sounder, electronic maps and more horsepower, to name just a few.

The pressure on the marine resources is therefore probably at least as severe as it was earlier. There are also several hundred thousand registered small boats along the coast. If each of these boats is responsible for a couple of self caught meals every year, it also has a large impact on the total resources of the sea.

The sea and the ocean have always been a common wealth, freely available to all who wish to increase their household's food supply with a long-awaited meal, or who wished to earn some money by fishing. It is still like this, the sea and the ocean are among our last sanctuaries.

Is the Seafood still Healthy?

When the papers constantly report about toxic pollutants along the coast, many people ask: How safe is it really to eat fish and shellfish caught in the skerries?
Are the crabs in Sørlandet safe and what about the fatty sea trout?

We all have been told that fish is healthy food. And it certainly is! Along most of the Southern Coast, the fish and shellfish are both safe and healthy. The rule of the thumb is that the further out in the sea the seafood is caught, the cleaner it is. But in the coastal areas where we have heavy industry, or in the harbours of the southern coastal towns, some of the fish and shellfish are affected by heavy metals and organotoxic pollutants. In simplified terms we can say that environmental pollutants are chemical stuff that are poisonous in small concentration, and which accumulate in the food chain and have a long decomposition time. The environmental toxic compounds often mentioned in this context are the dioxins, PAH, TBT, and PCB. These are unfamiliar and frightening terms for many people, and in this context it is sufficient to give some simple and general answers that are easy to remember.

The filets of all the fish that have been analysed are safe. And they include many of the most popular species such as cod, coalfish and pollock. Likewise, crab and lobster meat is safe in view of environmental pollutants, provided they are not caught in the harbour basin. Some dioxins are shown in crabmeat along the Telemark coast. The closer we get to Grenland fjords from the south west, the higher the concentration becomes. But it all depends on how often you eat shellfish. It should be quite safe to eat crab a few times a year.

When it comes to the dioxin levels in cod liver, generally the fish caught in the outermost parts of the coast are fine, except at Jomfruland, where the levels are somewhat high.

In the fjords near the harbour basins and in many fjords by towns along the Southern Coast, the values of environmental poison in liver are too high. Therefore, the Norwegian Food Safety Authority has provided guidelines for people living along the harbours. They are advised not to eat liver from fish caught in these areas. For more info: www.mattilsynet.no (The Norwegian Food Safety Authority).

Seafood is still among the healthiest you can eat. Not only because fish and shellfish are lean food, but because they contain high amounts of healthy proteins, minerals and trace elements. And above all, fish fat is supreme. The so-called omega 3 fatty acids found in seafood have a favourable effect on the development of the brain, rheumatism, aging, and vascular diseases, to name a few.

The team at Flødevigen today works with research and management advices within many disiplines:

- Monitoring and Assessment of the biologi cal values in the Coastal Zone.
- Environmental status in the North Sea, Skagerrak and the coastal zone
- Plant- and zooplankton in Skagerrak and the North Sea
- Coastal resources such as lobster, eel and cod
- Shrimp, herring, sprat and industrial fishing in Skagerrak and the North Sea
- Deep sea resources in North East Atlantic.

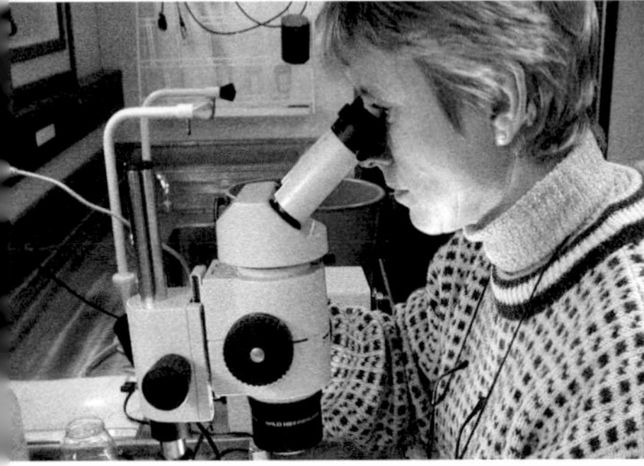

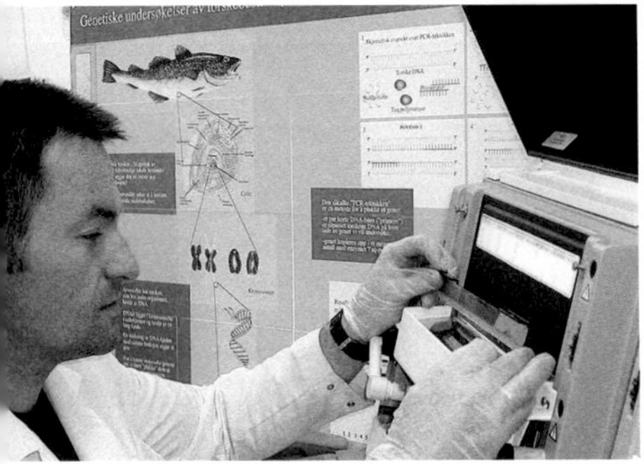

From the DNA lab

Institute of Marine Research

The Institute of Marine Research (IMR) in Flødevigen has over the years been a platform for varied research activities. For example, it was here the Norwegian fish farming venture began with hatching cod eggs.

The Institute's challenges are big, with research programmes along the coast of Norway as well as out at sea, in Skagerrak, the North Sea and in the Atlantic Ocean. In the last few years, the Institute of Marine Research has received particular attention, because the researchers from Flødevigen have led the international research project MAR-ECO. In the summer of 2004, MAR-ECO carried out a major exploratory voyage to the mid Atlantic ridge with FF "G.O Sars." On this voyage, a number of sensational discoveries were done, which stirred great media attention – both in Norway and many other countries.

The results from IMR DNA-labs in recent years have also caused sensation, and will probably change the way we manage future coastal cods in Norway.

Nevertheless, what most people associate with IMR-Flødevigen activities is information about algae (phytoplankton) with emphasis on harmful species. In co-operation with other institutions and important funding from the Norwegian Food Safety Authority, information on phytoplankton along the coast is reported weekly on the Internet.

The Institute of Marine Research at Flødevigen has among the longest time series in the world. For example, they have been using beach seine in the same way, the same place and same time, every year since 1919. Hundred and twenty stations from Hvaler to Kristiansand are monitored in order to study if the recruitment of commercial marine fishes is normal.

Spawn research with beach seine.

The Institute of Marine Research(IMR) in Flødevigen was established as early as in 1882 and is one of Norway's and Europe's oldest marine research stations. The research station is situated all the way out towards the sea at the island Hisøy outside Arendal, where it is perfectly situated for monitoring the Norwegian coastal current where it starts in the Skagerrak.

Institute of Marine Research, Flødevigen

Boa dragonfish

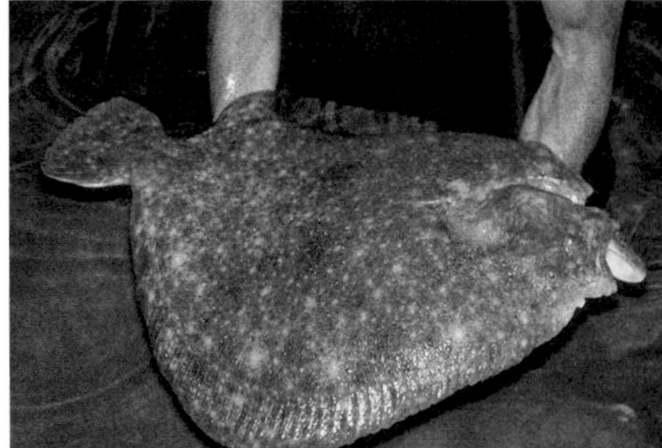

Turbot in the aquarium at the research station

Shrimps – the Perfect Summer Food

Few dishes can compete with shrimps. They are easy to serve and eat, as well as being tasty and healthy. Therefore, it is not strange that shrimps are a popular summer food.

When Professor Johan Hjort, in 1897, set out to study the marine life at the bottom of the outer areas of the Oslo fjord he never imagined that he would lay the foundation for the important trawl shrimp fisheries in the Skagerrak.

The professor was very surprised to find the deepwater shrimp *Pandalus borealis* at the bottom of the sea. The year after, he returned with his good Danish colleague C.G. Johannes Pettersen. They brought with them a homemade 'shrimp trawl', which they hoped could catch deep water shrimps. The question they asked was whether the shrimps could be exploited in practical fishing.

The results after the first trawls on the east and west side of the fjord were very encouraging. A novel fishing method was developed. Already the following year, they were joined by a little armada of local fishermen.

Trawl fishing for shrimps has in other words been going on for over a hundred years, and it still continues. The stock is in healthy condition and is a valuable source of excellent income for the fishers. All in all, more than 10 000 tons of shrimps are fished annually in the areas from Skagerrak to the Norwegian trench.

The shrimp stock is one of the few in Skagerrak

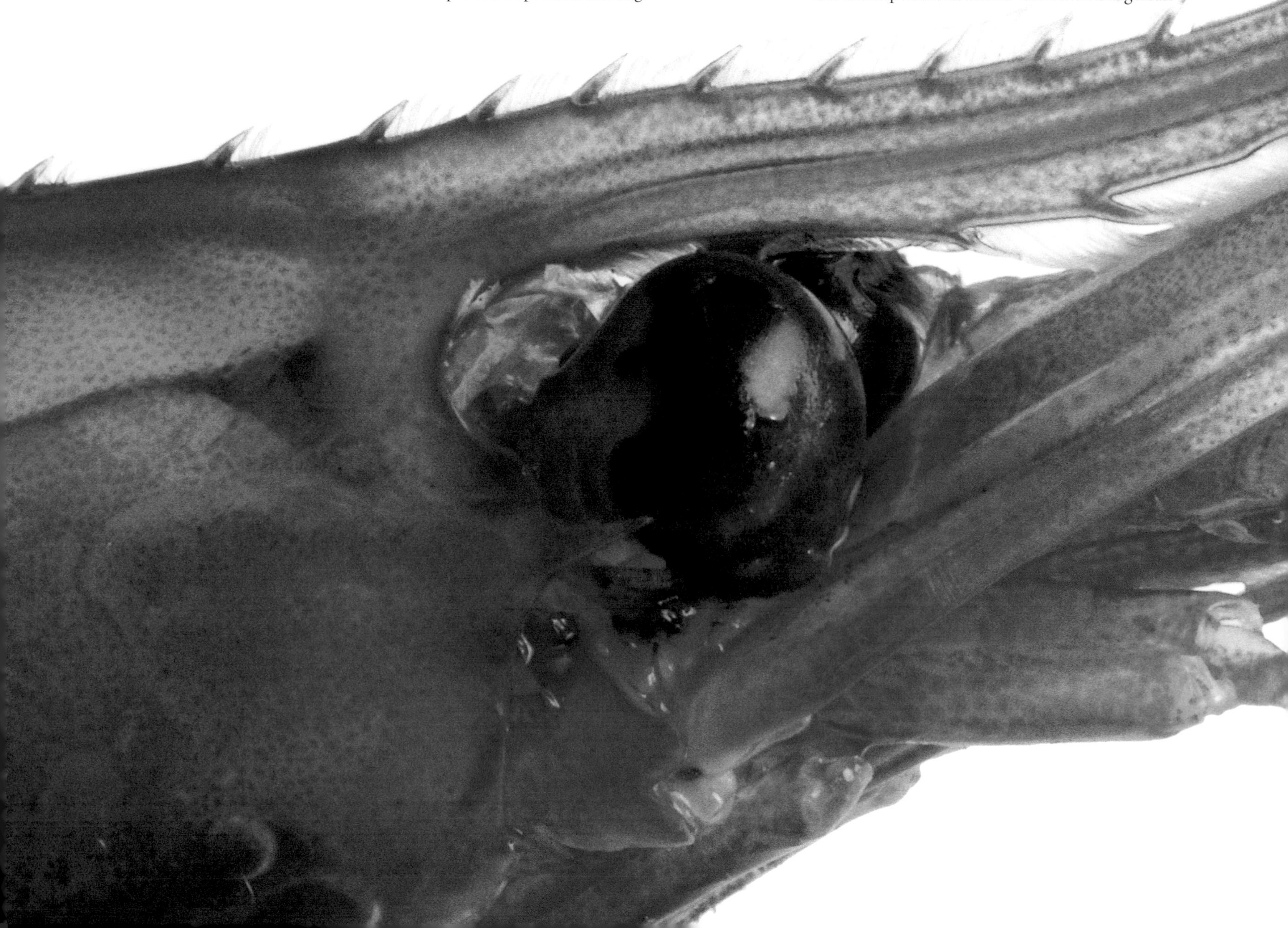

that has remained stable in the last 20-30 years. It has in fact probably increased, despite the intensive shrimp fishing in the area. It is difficult to determine the reason. It may be that many of the fish stocks in Skagerrak and the North Sea, such as cod that feed on shrimps, are heavily reduced and the shrimps are left in peace.

Did you know that:

- Researchers have no good methods to determine the age of shrimps and other shellfish above a certain age. In fish it is the otoliths that contain growth rings, which determine their age. Therefore, it is more difficult to obtain an overview of the shrimp stocks.

- The shrimps change sex when they reach a certain age. At first, the shrimps are males, but after two to two and a half years they change into females.

Shrimp trawler

Fishing with Net, Fish pots and Traps

Fishing equipments such as nets, pots and traps all have an interesting history. The first description of fishnets in Norway comes from the Rogaland coast, which tells about "ungodly" cod fishing in 1666.

Fishing cod with pots began around 1870. Ordinary wooden fish traps made with nets used for fishing crabs and lobster became common around 1930. While lobster traps have a long history, already in the sixteenth century there are mentions of a "log or basket that traps the lobster."

Trammel net is much utilised in Sørlandet. It catches fish effectively in shallow water. The net is international and used in large parts of the world. It consists of three layers, a small mesh, inner panel of netting is sandwiched between two outer layers of netting, which have a larger mesh size. In norwegian it is called "Troll net," and you can easily find out why when you pull up a net that has been out in the storm. You have to use a whole day to clean and get the 'troll' out of the net.

If using trammel net, it is important that the mesh size is not too small. Nets with too small meshes should be avoided because they trap large numbers of small cods.

Children like to fish with fish pots and traps, because it is always exciting to see what has been trapped during the night.
During summer, it is important to remember that there are depth limits for crab traps during the lobsters' conservation period (From January 1 to October 1 at 8 am).

You can not set out the traps in shallower areas than 25 meters.Pots can be put out in shallow water, but any lobsters taken in pots or nets must be set free.
The same applies to lobster fishing, whereby only lobster traps should be utilised.

The Norway Lobster

The Norway lobster does not get as much attention as its cousin the European lobster. But when it comes to taste, it is almost unsurpassed. Not surprisingly, norwegian lobster is a 'regular guest' on the menus of our most exclusive restaurants.

Its former name sand lobster is perhaps the most descriptive name for the Norway lobster, since it thrives best in sand and mud. Here we shall call it Norway lobster as it is commonly known.

The Norway lobster is a close relative to the more famous European lobster, but when it comes to their living habits and looks, these two species are extremely different. While Norway lobster is slim with a pink shell, European lobster is big and usually black. In addition, they have completely different habitats. Norway lobsters can be found at 50 to 200 meters depth. It preferes sand, clay and soft sea beds, while the European lobster lives in depths from 5 to 50 meters, and prefers rocky sea beds.

Norway lobsters dig themselves into the mud and can burrow deep holes. Particularly, one assumes that the fertile females hide in this manner, since so few of them are caught in the trawlers. Norway lobster is found both in the fjords and the open sea. But it is not only we who like to eat it. In the stomach of the deep water cod one often finds Norway lobster.

Catching Norway lobsters in traps has become very popular among hobby fishers, who have started catching them in fjords at about 40 to 60 meters deep. They seldom catch many at a time, but enough for their enjoyment.

Norway lobsters live in soft bed areas where they can find both food and shelter, usually at the edge of so-called deep water basins or at the thresholds. Common lobster traps with small openings are suitable, but the meshes in the pot must be small.

The Norway lobster which is sold at fishmongers along the Southern Coast comes for the most part from the crawfish trawlers. Six hundred tons are caught annually in Skagerrak, effectively performed from boats with two to three crew members.

SAGA RIVER

Lobster Fishing

Lobster fishing has been extremely important for Sørlandet for more than 300 years. Earlier, lobster fishing was coastal fishermen's main source of income. Today, increasingly more people fish lobster purely for pleasure.

In the beginning, around year 1500, lobsters were picked with a peg. They must have been available in vast numbers. No wonder that the Dutch established their own freight ships to transport the catch to the Netherlands. Later documents show that a total of 2,5 millions of lobsters were caught in one year – and that was not even a record!

The choice of bait and location are subject to long discussions when it comes to lobster fishing. While one fisher will swear to salted fish as bait – to keep the crabs away – another will only use fresh bait, and the third prefers rotten baits. The smell, or rather stench, of fermented fish is indescribable. It sets new standards for bad smell. The most important thing is probably to place the pots where the lobster is, since it is more or less a place bound creature.

Desirable and expensive, it is a delicacy everyone knows about. Unfortunately the prices are too high for everyone to be able to afford the sweet and tasty meat. Maybe that is precisely why the southerners are so eager to get their 'webbed toes' into the water at 8 am 1st of October, the moment the lobster fishing season begins.

In her eminent cook book, Henriette Schønberg Erken gives the following advice: "The lobster should feel heavy in the hand – if it is light it is watery. The medium large ones are always best. A medium large lobster is preferable because the meat has a finer taste."

Lobsters over a kilo are not common. If the pots are set out in deeper water the chances of catching larger lobsters increase. But take only a couple, because the big ones are vital for producing lobster juveniles. Large fertile females can carry up to 20 000 to 30 000 eggs.

If on a fine autumn day you meet a southerner gazing at the sea and find it difficult to attract his attention, do not be offended. He just has an important thing on his mind: The start of the lobster fishing season.

Few traditions have been preserved as well as lobster fishing along the coast. For many people the season starts on the first day of October, decidedly the highpoint of the season. Family life and work is organized such that 'pater familias' can set out his traps and ensure the family's lobster feasts.

All those who take their lobster fishing seriously are meticulous about the minimum size. Lobsters that are not the permitted size – either too small or too big – are thrown back into the sea again. In other words, only lobsters measuring minimum 24 cm from tail to head are taken.

The European Lobster

European lobsters are mainly found along the coast of the North Sea and Skagerrak. In the east, they are in the area towards Kattegat, westwards to Shetland and northwards to Tromsø. In addition, there is a special population of lobster in Tysfjord, and there are actually lobsters also in the Mediterranean!

European lobsters have always been in demand, and during the whole period after WWII until the 60s, Norway was number one in lobster fishing in Northern Europe.

The incomes from lobster fishing were fundamental for many professional fishers on the coast. In this period, the catches were between 600 and 1000 tons per year. Today only 50 tons are delivered through governmental trade agencies. Even though the taxation system has changed and much of the lobster does not reach the market, we lose millions each year when the lobster stock is so dramatically reduced.

The lobster stock is present at a historical low, following a continuous decline since the first years after WWII and up to the new millennium. The last two to three years however, there has been some positive development. Many things seem to indicate that increasing the minimum size in 1992 from 22 to 24 cm, is beginning to show results. It will be interesting to follow the development ahead, because our coast is the closest we get to a lobster paradise – we only need to manage the resources properly.

In more than a hundred years, the researchers in Norway and in Europe have thoroughly examined the sea in search of the undiscovered fourth stage of the lobster. They have managed to find the first, second and third stages of the lobster, that is the newly hatched larvae which in summer swim around in five to ten meters deep water on the coast. But where the lobster larvae head to at a further stage is still a mystery. Some fishers have reported seeing small lobsters swimming close to shore almost in a school. Other say they have taken fertile lobsters all the way down at 100 meters. Perhaps the secret lies buried in the deep?

Establishing lobster reserves may be a way of increasing the stock. The results from lobster reserves from Lysekil in Sweden and other places indicate that it will take about ten years to increase the local stock, if an area is preserved and protected completely.

However, protecting the whole lobster stock for ten years in Norway is not quite feasible, because the political opposition is much too strong.

Marine protected areas (MPAs) are internationally popular fields of research at present. As expected, many stationary fish and shellfish populations quickly increase the stocks when the areas are protected.

The density of lobsters in the Swedish reserve is 6,3 lobsters per sea acre. Along the Norwegian coast we have vast sea areas. That means that in an ordinary coastal community there may be place for perhaps thirty to fifty thousand lobsters. It is about time we utilise this possibility to increase economic growth in the local communities along the coast.

The lobster lives at the bottom of the sea and thrives on stony and rocky beds. In the big rocky screes it finds good shelters where it can stay all day. First at nightfall, it ventures out in search of food which consists mostly of shells, mussels and sea urchins that crushes with its powerful claws.

Lobster spawn
Through experiments in aquariums we know that the fourth stage lobster larvae move to the bottom of the sea. But we do not know where they settle. The little lobster apparently 'disappears' for two years. Then it suddenly pops up in the pots of the eel fishers in summer. These individuals are about seven to eight centimetres long.

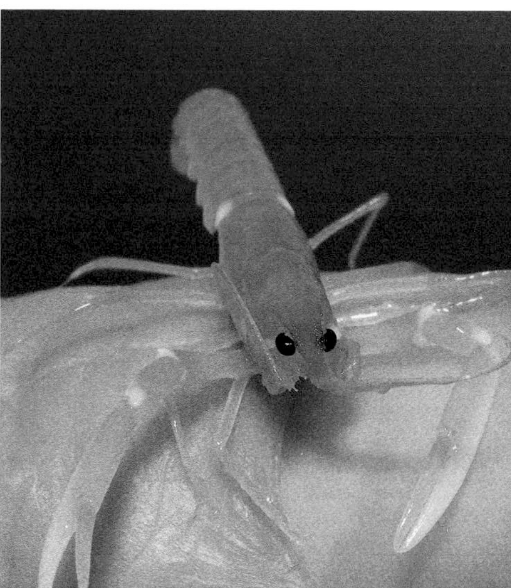

The lumpfish larvae are well developed and after a few days manage on their own. It remains a couple of years in the kelp forest, often sucked to the bottom of the sea or to stones or seaweeds.

Lumpfish

Lumpfish pulls in towards the coast in spring, where the kelp forest is a cherished dwelling place. Female lumpfish is bluish grey, while the male becomes characteristically red under the belly during the spawning period.

Lumpfish has a powerful sucker disc under its belly, used for attaching itself to stones and rocks at the bottom of the sea. It is a good tool for the female when it lays eggs and for the male when it guards them. If you place a lumpfish on a slippery surface, it will suck on to it and hold its own weight. Talk about power surplus!

Until recently, it was thought that the lumpfish lived most of its life in the shallow waters along the coast. Now, new research has revealed that the lumpfish spends great parts of the year out in the open sea, surrounded by herrings, mackerel and salmon.

And we who thought that a torpedo shaped body and proper camouflage with dark back and light belly was a precondition for surviving at sea. On the other hand, the lumpfish does not have many enemies. It requires quite a big mouth to swallow a fish shaped like ball.

The lumpfish can change colour according to its environment. The fish to the right has the colour of kelp forest. The fish to the left has been in a fish basin.

"Oh, how sweet," children say spontaneously when they see a lump fish for the first time.
The adults are more fascinated by the fact that such round and seemingly harmless fish can manage to survive out in the sea, without sharp teeth or speed.

Limfjord caviar is made from lumpfish roe. The biggest females can provide nearly a litre of this attractive caviar. During spring, there is active fishing for females along the whole coast of Norway.

Catfish

Catfish

The catfish is both thick skinned and bigmouthed. But despite this rough exterior it lives a very peaceful life. Most of the time, it remains quietly under a stone or in a cove. When searching for food, it swims quietly around and gathers shells, mussels and crabs, which it crushes in its mouth with its exceptionally powerful jaws.

The catfish is not afraid of anything and it is not easily irritated. But be careful. Once a catfish is goaded, you are in trouble, and if it bites you it will not let go. Because its jaws are so strong you can place the fish on the edge of the boat where it bites on, and stays for a long time with its body straight out.

There are three species of catfish in Norway. It is the common catfish, spotted wolffish and northern wolffish. They are found both in shallow water and deeper in the sea. Along the Southern Coast you find only catfish.

Catfish is one of the few fishes with internal fertilization. The six millimetre eggs are laid in a lump at the bottom of the sea, and each lump can contain anything between five to ten thousand eggs. The male guards the eggs by curling itself around the egg mass until they hatch.

Catfish is easily recognizable. It has a large catlike head and powerful teeth, hence its name in many countries including Sweden and Denmark.

In spite of its scary looks, catfish is a splendid food, popular in restaurants.

Both catfish and the spotted wolffish are considered as exquisite delicacies. The Northern wolffish on the other hand is completely inedible.

The skull of a catfish

A ribbon made from the skin of a spotted wolffish

Sea Urchins and Sea Cucumber – Delicious!

Did you know that the sea urchins can be eaten raw and that the roe is among the most expensive seafood products of the World?

In 1995, as much as 110 000 ton of sea urchins were harvested worldwide. The Japanese are among the biggest consumers of sea urchins. Maybe we should also taste this exquisite delicacy?

The sea urchins are from the same family as the starfish. The majority have long spikes on their shells and suction discs on their feet, which enables them to move quite fast. The spikes are used as defence against the catfish, crabs and other creatures who eat sea urchins.

It is the roe that makes the sea urchin attractive, located just under the skull resembling five small orange pieces. The roe functions as the sea urchins' energy storage, and when spawning time approaches, tiny eggs are formed in the roes of the female urchin and milk in the male. When the eggs and the milk mix, small larvae are hatched, which float around in the water before settling down at the bottom of the sea with their small suction feet.

We have four different species of sea urchins in Norway. The most common one is the Green sea urchin. There are however very few sea urchins along the Southern Coast compared to the Western Coast and the Northern Coast.

The sea urchins have grazed much of the kelp forest, from the Trøndelag coast and northwards. In such razed areas, the Norwegian Sea urchins have very little roe because many of them have too little food.

Researchers have begun feeding the sea urchins to make the roe more attractive as food. In this test, they have developed a special food for the sea urchins. The food consists of fish skin and seaweed, and they add a natural colouring that enhances the colour of the roe.

The sea urchins are picked alive and placed in a large container full of water. When they have been fed for two months, they contain twice as much roe – enough to send them to Japan by plane, where they are sold as a delicacy. Perhaps it is worth tasting it in Norway, too.

The Sea cucumber
Parastichopus tremulus
can become up to 50 cm long and is a very common catch in shrimp trawlers along the Southern Coast. It belongs to a family of sea urchins with soft, cucumber shaped body and calcareous scales on its skin. The mouth is surrounded by small tentacles. Of the 1100 or so species of sea cucumbers that exist about 35 are found in Norwegian waters. Sea cucumber is actually a tasty seafood – similar to oysters. The way to prepare it is to clean, cook and dry. In China, it is usual to soak the dried sea cucumbers before serving. The Chinese highly value the sea cucumber as health food and aphrodisiac - and some consider it as the elixir of youth. A gift of the 'finest sea cucumbers' is not uncommon to give when visiting people in China.

Red sea urchin

Sea cucumber

Seeing under Water

Sørlandet with its exposed coastline, wide archipelago and varied fjords has much to offer hobby divers. But for an optimal diving experience it is important to know when the visibility is at its best, and where to find the finest underwater fauna and flora.

When it comes to visibility, it is seldom a good time during the spring bloom, between March and the beginning of May. Later the diving conditions vary depending on the direction of the wind. After a few days off-shore wind (wind from the North/Northwest) the visibility can be good. Accordingly, a longer period of onshore wind can result in lousy visibility. The best so-called safe periods are midsummer, late autumn and winter.

Night diving in kelp forests can be a fantastic experience. Meadows of kelp forests (*Laminaria hyperborea*) grow on rocky bases in these areas, from three meters deep down to about 20 meters. With a little experience you can find the forest with an echo sounder. Although the kelps are not as tall as the ones in the West – and the North Coast, they are part of a vital vegetation zone along the whole Southern Coast of Norway.

The kelp forest is considered as one of the most productive ecosystems in the world, with an enormous primary production. To swim in kelp forest is always fascinating, but at night it is particularly exciting. The kelp forests are colonized by a number of plants and animals that find both their food and shelter there. At night, they emerge from their hiding places, neither frightened nor wary.

There is a myriad of life among the kelps. With a good torch you can see lobsters, crabs, great spider crabs, isopods, amphipods, gobies, goldsinny, ballan wrasse, corkwing wrasse, rock cook and cuckoo wrasse, to name some. At the bottom you find starfish and brittlestar, cod fish and the odd pollock hovering just above the sea bed. Beautiful red algae grow on the stalks of the kelps. The most common are sea beech, sea oak and dulse.

If you like excitement, it is possible to take a Hawaii sling with you when diving. At the end of November and beginning of December the large cods are gathered to taste the goodies in the kelp forest.

Catfish 'hunting' in May is also popular among divers. In Risør there is a special Catfish festival during that period, when the catfish retreats to shallower waters. And in the Risør skerries they have put in cement pipes to lure in the fish. The Risør underwater club, who is the proud organizer of the event, also makes sure that the catch is prepared according to all culinary rules. They serve the tastiest catfish dishes ever. Incidentally, the catfish is relatively hard to catch when it has reached a certain size, and you must know what you are doing if the 'hunt' is to be safe. Its jaws are incredibly powerful and that fish can bite!

Flounder and one arm of a starfish

Foreign Species

The introduction of foreign species is a global problem. An increasing number of marine species are transported around the world to new habitats. In Norway, many of the foreign species have arrived via the fish farming or shipping industries. We have a number of newly introduced species in Norway, the red king crab and the American lobster being the most famous.

In 2001, the spread of the poisonous algae *Chattonella* cf. verruculosa caused great losses for the fish farming industry at Flekkefjord. Almost 1000 tons of farmed fish, with a value of NOK 25 million, died. The algae known from Japanese waters, was probably brought here in the ballast water emptied in our sea.

Japanese wireweed was first observed along the Southern Coast in 1984. The weed spread to Europe following the import of Pacific oysters for farming. Through the English Channel it has now spread both to the south and to the north. Today Japanese wireweed is common along the whole of the Southern Coast and to the North along the Western Coast, where in some places it is choking bays and harbours.

The red macroalgae, *Gracilaria vermicullophylla*, which is quickly spreading along the Swedish coast, is an introduced species that could have had a negative effect on the eelgrass in our waters. Tests performed in the Swedish waters show a dramatic decrease in the amount of eelgrass in the last 20 years.

St. Peter's fish

Seabass has become very popular among hobby fishers, and it seems like it is here to stay. Not all so-called foreign species seem to be potentially harmful. The reason that these species appear along our coasts is higher average sea temperatures in recent years. Visiting fish from warmer climates are therefore not an unusual sight, and they are perhaps strictly speaking not foreign species, but species that have increased their range northwards due to climate changes. The European seabass belongs to this group.

Mullet is a small fish that also appears along the Southern Coast from time to time. Although in our waters it is a small and foreign fish, it is much bigger in the Mediterranean, and was extremely appreciated in Roman times.

St. Peter's fish has become quite a common catch in the shrimp trawlers in Norway. Divers have also seen them in shallow areas. Rising water temperatures in the summers is considered to be the main reasons for these frequent visits from our south sea guests to Sørlandet.

St. Peter's fish is an interesting fish. It is round like a flounder, but swims right side up with large breast fins. The characteristic and easily recognizable black spot on its side is supposed to be St. Peter's fingerprint. He left his fingerprint on the fish when he lifted it. Whether St. Peter wanted to put it straight into the pan is rather doubtful, since the fish survived the encounter. But without doubt, St. Peter's fish is an exquisite food – not sold in fish shops in Norway, so far.

Japanese wireweed

European seabass

Mullet

A Lobster from America

In the autumn of 1999, the lobster fishers were in truth surprised when they found two unusual lobsters in their traps in Oslofjord. They were experienced fishers and knew something was wrong. Therefore, they delivered the lobsters to the Aquarium in Drøbak, which sent them on to the Institute of Marine Research and the Aquarium in Bergen. The conclusion was clear and sensational: The first American lobsters were caught in Norway.

It is relatively easy to see the difference between a typical European lobster and an American one. The European lobster has smaller and longer carapax than its American cousin, which has a broad and short carapax. The colour of European lobster is usually jet black. The most common colour of American lobster is reddish brown/green. Moreover, the European lobster seldom has a rostrum with spikes pointing downwards, which is a typical characteristic in the American. In addition, the European lobster has a white spot on its cheek and several white patches or spots on its head and claws, which the American lobster very seldom has. Finally, we should mention that the American lobster is much more volatile than the placid European. Nevertheless, it must be emphasized that the European lobster's appearance can vary tremendously, and requires a trained eye to determine its species. In certain doubtful cases, it is even necessary to take a DNA test in order to establish the species with confidence.

American lobsters mainly live on the east coast of USA and Canada, where they have large, but strictly regulated lobster fishery. Because of their great numbers, American lobster is exported to Europe. As in other places in Europe, it is allowed to import live American lobsters. However, it is prohibited to set them out into the sea. Probably that is what has happened. People have put them in the sea to keep them alive until they are ready to eat them, but then the lobsters have escaped accidentally.

Until now, there have been twelve documented (DNA-tested) sightings of American lobster along the coast of Norway. The lobsters have all been between 24 and 30 cm, and many of them have had an elastic band round the claws, or marks left by elastic bands. This proves that they have not been in the sea for long. Most American lobsters have been caught in Oslofjord, or along the coast of Skagerrak, but American lobsters have also been caught in both Hordaland and in Ålesund region.

What worries the researchers is that the American lobster has the potential to roam. However, until now there has been no observation of small American lobsters, which may indicate that for the moment it does not seem to have spawned in Norwegian waters. It will be interesting to follow this in the years to come.

The risk of spreading disease and infections that are alien to European lobster is one of the threats often mentioned in this connection. One example is the disease gaffkemia that the American lobster is immune to, but which is a hundred percent deadly for European lobsters.

The imported female lobsters are also usually fertilized in America and will be able to spawn several thousands of eggs in Norwegian waters if set out in the sea. In such a small sea as the Skagerrak, a foreign species such as the American lobster will be able to spread fast once it gets a foothold. We do not know how many American lobsters have escaped in the Norwegian waters. We hope the last one is caught!

American lobster (to the left) and European lobster (to the right).

American lobsters have antennules with a few spikes facing downwards.

European lobsters have antennules with spikes facing upwards.

Seal Invasion

In recent years, flocks of common seals have taken residence in the archipelago in autumn after the summer tourists have left. Some places, particularly along the Telemark coast, there have been reported flocks of 15 to 20 seals.

The seals have occupied the outermost rocks and also settled inside the fjords. Although they are only a few, their numbers are increasing.

Seals are widely spread from Kola to Portugal. The smallest seals live along the whole coast of Norway and are relatively place bound.
The seals can hold their breath for up to 6-7 minutes. They are fantastic swimmers and as elegant in the water as they are clumsy on land. The baby seals are born towards the end of June, beginning of July. The seal eats only fish and is therefore often considered a pest by the locals. It is permitted to hunt seal in parts of Norway, when the stocks become too big.

Seals are shy animals and keep to the coastal areas where it is easy for them to find food, and where the skerries are wide with low islets and small islands. They prefers places with few houses and few people.

We know for sure that the seals on the Southern Coast have 'roamed' in either from Østfold or Sweden. On the west coast of Sweden and in Østfold, the seal stock is relatively large and expanding quickly. Only in Hvaler there are about 400 to 500 animals, compared to the coast of Sørlandet that has less than 200 seals.
It is not that many years ago (2002), that more than a thousand seals in Sweden, Østfold and the Southern Coast died of seal pest.

The seal eats fish, a serious concern for people living along the coast who are worried that the seal will eat up the local fish stocks. Even respectable newspapers write that the seals eat tremendous amounts of fish. Scientific data show that the seal eats about two to four kilos of fish per day. This means that the fifteen seals living outside Lyngør eat about twelve to fifteen tons of fish a year.

Worse is that the quality of the fish deteriorates with seals in the sea, because the fish become infected with roundworms. Moreover, the seals also take some salmon and trout on their way up the river to spawn. Nevertheless, not everyone likes this negative focus on the seals.

For many people the seals are a fascinating experience. It is undoubtedly fantastic to see a flock of seals lazing about on a rock, and watch them elegantly slide into the sea if one gets too close

People who are often out at sea along the Southern Coast report seeing seals more frequently than before. Is the seal stock growing? Many people want to know why. And is it really such a problem with seals along the coast as we are made to believe?

Common seal

The Sea Plants

Seaweeds

By sea plants we mean both the microscopic plankton algae, as well as stationary algae at the bottom of the sea. In addition, there are flowering plants such as the eelgrass that grows both in sandy and muddy beds.

The benthic algae are divided into three groups: red algae, green algae and brown algae – many are easily recognizable by their colour. The largest and best known algae are usually called seaweeds.

Seaweeds grow in the shallow end of the shore with species such as knotted wrack and bladder wrack, while the kelp grows in deeper waters – from 1 – 20 meters deep along the Southern Coast. Sea tangle, oarweed and sugar kelp are well-known species.

Like the plants on land, seaweeds also need light. In addition, they need a solid 'anchoring point' – often on a rocky bottom.

Although seaweeds are large plants, they comprise only a fraction of the total plant production in the sea. The production is dominated by plankton.

THE LIGHT SHINES IN THROUGH THE WATERS WHERE
THE SEAWEEDS UTILISE IT IN THEIR PHOTOSYNHESIS
– JUST LIKE THE GREEN PLANTS ON LAND

Eelgrass

Eelgrass is a marine vein plant that is normally found in shallow bays and coves in the Pacific Ocean, the Atlantic Ocean, round the British Isles, as well as along the whole coast of Norway up to Russia. Eelgrass differs from seaweed by the fact that it has a root system that it uses to absorb nutrition and to stay put.

We have two eelgrass species in Norway: common eelgrass (*Zostera marina*) and dwarf eelgrass (*Zostera noltii*). The latter is a rare species and is on the Red List of Threatened Species.

In Norway, the area where the eelgrass grows is not mapped well, but the biodiversity associated with the eelgrass is examined in some places. The eelgrass plant usually grows on a flat bottom in partially protected bays and coves with soft seabed, sand, gravel or sandy mud.

In our waters, the plants are from 20 to 100 cm tall and grow in depths from one to seven meters. Eelgrass is often scattered about, but in certain areas there are larger, interconnected zones.

If you wonder where to find eelgrass, find out where the fishers place their eel traps. Because the eel thrives best in the eelgrass where there is ample food and adequate shelter.

The eelgrass is decreasing in all of Europe and many countries monitor these habitations carefully, since they have great importance for the biological production and diversity in the coastal regions.

Over fertilization of the coastal waters are considered among the main reasons for the disappearance of the eelgrass. Sludge sediments from docks and seawater pipes lead to the destruction of the eelgrass. Paradoxically, according to the law, the environmental authorities, the fishing department or harbour authorities are not allowed to prohibit dumping of sludge by using the protection of eelgrass as an argument. The fact that this is a key issue marine biologically is not taken into consideration – yet. On the other hand, if the area gets polluted, the case is handled differently. Then according to the law it is forbidden to sludge. Try to make heads or tails of it, if you can!

Introduction of foreign species can also be a threat to the eelgrass. In the Mediterranean Sea the spread of the introduced green algae *Caulerpa taxifolia*, has had a negative effect on the Neptun grass (*Posidonia oceanica*), which is a type of sea grass. Japanese wireweed which now appears in large amounts along the coast of Southern Norway, tand he red algae *Gracilaria vermicullophylla* that is quickly spreading along the Swedish West coast, are both introduced species that may have negative effects on the eelgrass.

Once eelgrass has disappeared from an area, it will have limited possibility to take root again, since it has poor spreading ability.

The eelgrass meadows are among the best habitat for small cods and are the sea trout's favourite feeding place. But that is not all! Few other natural habitat in the sea have a higher biodiversity than the eelgrass community, in which you find a teeming life.

Eel

Seaweed – Sea Snacks

Most Norwegians seem to have problems imagining that seaweed has anything to do with food. But nearly all those who dare taste it are amazed of the delicious taste. Seaweed is moreover full of both vitamins and minerals. In Asia, seaweed is an important ingredient in sushi.

Seaweeds contain chlorophyll and are a primary producer in the sea through their photosynthesis, just like green plants are on land. The production in the kelp forest for example is extremely high and in many ways can be compared to an underwater rain forest.

Like the rain forest, the kelp forest teems with life, between the stems, the 'roots' and the leaves.

Trawling for kelp has been a big industry in Norway for a number of years. This takes place from Rogaland to Trøndelag, with the help of gigantic underwater mowers. In 2005, 160 000 tons of kelp were harvested. Although this is only a tiny fraction of the standing kelp biomass on the Norwegian coast there is an ongoing debate whether this activity is reducing the fish stock.

Today, kelp is used in the preservation industry, because it contains alginate. This can be used as thickening agent in soft ice cream and many other food stuff. Food with E-number intervals 400-408, contains algae matters.

To take a trip round this natural larder and pick algae for seaweed soup is a seldom activity for most Norwegians. During the Viking period, they gathered a certain type of red algae – dulse – which was dried and stored in barrels and utilised as vegetables and snacks.

If you have had seaweed soup with ballan wrasse, you have probably experienced that it is both tasty and different.

A number of edible algae grow along the whole coastline. The Chinese and Japanese have been aware of this fact for a long time and both use algae in cooking. They love seaweed in all its varieties. In Asian waters algae is grown and harvested on large scale.

The following sorts of algae can be recommended:

- Sea lettuce – with its fresh green colour
- Knotted wrack – the light shoots
- Sugar kelp – fresh young leaves
- The red algae dulse – grows on kelp stems

Algae that grow in the outer skerries where the water is fresh and clean are the best.

Preparations:: The coarse algae must be cooked for about 45 minutes in water and a little salt until they become tender. Sea lettuces and knotted wrack can be used raw in salads.

Seaweed has been used as animal fodder

Finger kelp, Oarweed

Bladder wrack

Knotted wrack

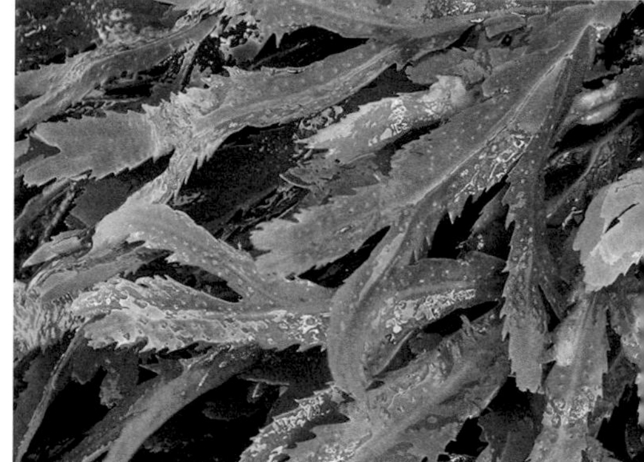
Toothed wrack

Sugar kelp

Sea lettuce

Dulse

On Rocks and Beaches

Coastal Landscape

The landscape in Sørlandet is very old, and very little of the surface we see today has changed in one billion years. At that time, there was no life on land and only primitive life in the sea. The finishing touch was put on the landscape during the ice age, when the glaciers and waters from the melted ice brought along loosened rocks, eroded valleys, polished the rocks and filled creeks and crevices with sand.

Out in the sea the glaciers left behind a large moraine, which follows the Southern Coast.

Most of the ancient landscape is under water now, but some 'peaks' stick out and create small skerries and shallow 'under-water' banks. Closer to shore, these peaks are formed as islets and islands. Closest to shore, the landscape contains larger islands. Inside these islands you find attractive small fjords for example Blindleia at Lillesand and Sørlandsleia from Lyngør to Arendal.

THE SANDY BEACHES ARE USUALLY SITUATED ON THE INNER SIDES OF THE ISLANDS, BECAUSE THE SEA MOVES THE SAND WHERE THE WAVES ARE GENTLE.

The Moraine, Raet

Towards the end of the ice age, about ten thousand years ago, a huge gravel ridge was deposited at the point where the inland ice ended. Imagine the pictures you have seen from the Antarctic, with massive ice walls towards the sea. The sea was 50 to 100 meters higher than it is today and the glaciers deposited masses of sand and gravel on the bottom of the sea and created a moraine.

In Sørlandet, we find this moraine at the continuation of the gravel ridge that goes out into the sea at Mølen near Larvik. Further south we find parts of the moraine in Jomfruland, and pebble beaches in Målen, Tromlingene, the outer side of Tromøya and Jerkholmen, which are also part of this enormous gravel ridge. Finally the moraine joins the land in Hasseltangen at Fevik – beneath beautiful beech woods. The moraine continues further inland towards the southwest.

The biologically productive sea beds – with its abundance of fish along the Southern Coast is also a part of the moraine.

When walking on the pebble beaches, you have perhaps noticed that there are many types of pebbles. When the ice moved towards south and west, it took along the stones. The glaciers that drifted with the currents towards southwest along the coast 10 000 years ago, also carried rocks. The pebble beaches have therefore stones that come from places further east, but never from the west.

Jomfruland

Bare Rocks

Did you know that dark bare rocks consist of softer minerals than the lighter rocks? As a result, the dark rocks become more finely polished than the light ones. Dark rocks also keep the heat better and are therefore preferable for sunbathing.

Many people know that the bare rocks along the coast are the result of being scrubbed clean by ice. The gravel and stones that moved under the glaciers acted like giant sand machines and created irrestible bare rocks.

The fine smooth shapes of the rocks are ideal for resting and sunbathing on lazy summer days.

The reason that we so seldom find bare rocks inland is that during the last ten thousand years they have been gradually covered with vegetation. The roots from the plants loosened the rich minerals, while the remaining hard minerals made the surface rough and uneven in the process. Only rocks that have been protected from roots have retained their smooth, polished surface.

It is only a "short while" ago that the land along the coast emerged from the waters. Consequently the smooth rocks have been protected by sea since the ice age. Today, the waves and harsh weather prevent vegetation from taking root.

You may have noticed that you always find sandy beaches on the inner side of the islands, while on the outer side it is more stony? The sea washes sand and small gravel over the island and leaves them on the inner side, where the waves are not so forceful. Just a few meters off the pebble beach on the outside the bottom of the sea is also sandy. This sand is brought in by the sea and deposited where the waves are gentler. Some years, the waves wash the sand over the pebbles and the result is an exotic and fresh beach.

The landscape in Sildeodden at Fie southwest of Risør is an excititing study for those who are interested in geology and aesthetics. There are clear traces of disintegration and scouring marks. These traces indicate that during the ice age the glaciers moved over the rocks like giant sand machines.

The coastal landscape of Southern Norway is beautiful. There are no high peaks or deep valleys, but instead you have welcoming, smoothly polished rocks and small islands. Nevertheless, that does not make it geologically less interesting. The stone formations you see on the islands and islets you visit reveal that also here powerful geological processes have been taking place.

Just a billion years ago, there were enormous mountain ranges in the area now known as the Southern Coast. Deep down this mountain was so hot that the stones became soft and elastic creating strange formations. The results are common sights along the Southern Coast.

Potholes are smooth, round depressions that were created by the rotation of stones caused by water. Most of the potholes in Norway were created towards the end of the ice age – about ten thousand years ago.

In the old days, people believed that these potholes were created by trolls or giants.

Potholes can be found in many places, but they are easiest to find where the river runs into the sea, and on the outer rocks along the coast where the sea has washed away the vegetation and soil. At Jomfruland and Lyngør, there are some fine potholes, but none of them can match up to the big and beautiful pothole at Sild by Fie outside Risør. It is six meters in diameter and five meters deep, and is situated right at the edge of the sea – a perfect pool built by nature herself.

The landscape in Sild is a fascinating study for those interested in geology. There are clear traces of scouring marks and disintegration. In this area, the ice age glaciers glided over the rocks making them smooth and round – perfect for sunbathing, but difficult to swim from because of the big waves breaking on the rocks. But it is great to bathe in the big pothole, also for children who can swim.

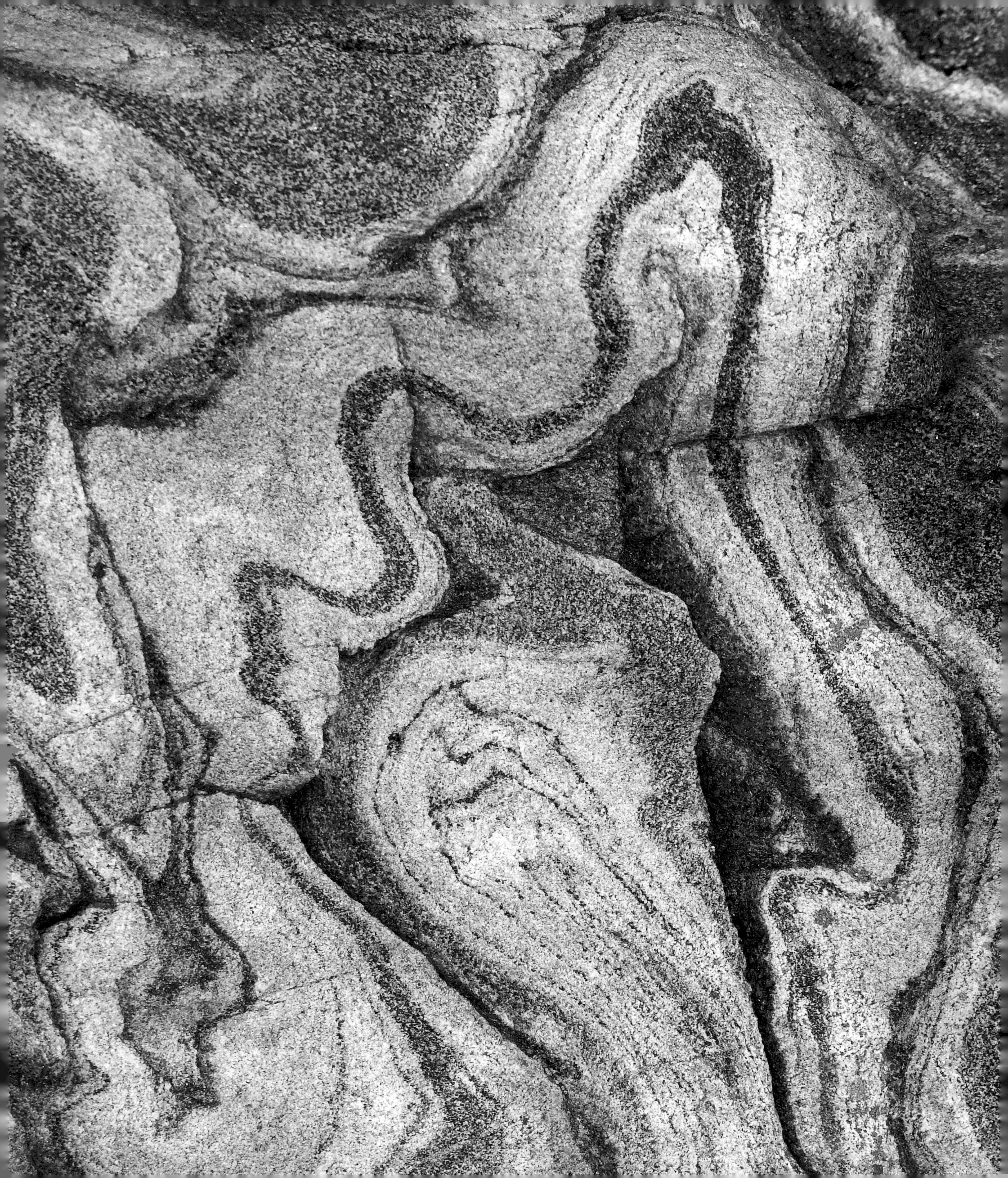

The Coastal Plants

The coastal plants decorate the chinks and fissures in the rocks, between pebbles and along the sandy beaches of the Southern Coast. Just before summer, the beach carnations and the ladies' delight appear like fresh splashes of colour on the rocks. They are later joined by a number of more or less striking plants.

The coastal climate has both its advantages and disadvantages for the plants growing there. The greatest advantage is that there are very few trees and plants which "steal" the sunlight. The temperatures are also relatively stable, because the sea retains the heat when the temperatures rise, and releases heat when temperatures sink. The sea's ability to regulate heat, combined with the effects of lukewarm water brought along with the Gulf Stream from southern latitudes, result in mild winters. When the autumn and winter storms rage flinging seaweeds on land, it does not take very long before bacteria, fungi and creepy-crawlies begin to wear down the marine plants. The nutrients that are thus released turn into fertilizer and nourishment for the land plants.

The greatest disadvantages for the coastal plants are of course lack of freshwater, high temperatures and dehydration. From this point of view, the coastal plants do not have an easy life. Only the best adjusted species manage to hang on and survive.

The most specialized coastal plants live closest to the shore. The further you get from the beach and the ebb line, the more 'land bound' the plant life becomes.

Those plants that manage to store or acquire water even under unfavourable conditions, and at the same time retain water when the temperature rises, are the winners among the coastal plants. They are either succulents or plants that exude wax which clogs the surface of the leaves.

Many beach plants are succulents. This means that the leaves and stems swell up and store water – almost like cacti. You see it clearly if you study the cost leaves on the biting stonecrops. If you squeeze the leaves liquid will seep out.

Sedum Rosea is a more outstanding succulent. It has thick, fleshy leaves on a chunky stem. Usually the leaves are green, but on the islands at the outpost of the archipelago it is exposed to scorching sun and the leaves are therefore often wine red.

Beach carnations and ladies' delights decorate the creeks and crevices in the rocks.

The caprifole is the county flower of Aust-Agder County. You can find it nearly everywhere in the archipelago. The plant climbs majestically up the cliff sides, tree trunks and stone fences. In the evening the beautiful flowers exude a delightfully sweet scent, almost like an exquisite perfume. If the winter is mild, the caprifole can grow even on bare rocks, as long as it finds a little sheltered crevice.

The bloody cranesbill prefers sheltered southerly slopes, protected from sun and wind. It is called as such not only because of its flower that can often be bluish purple, but its stem which is crimson after the flower blooms.

The Dog rose grows on bushes and thickets between polished rocks. There are several familiar dog roses with red, pink or white flowers. In autumn, you can pick the rose hips full of vitamin C.

Sea kale is a living proof of the nutritious soil of pebble beaches. The large sea kales can become almost one meter tall – a confirmation that the shoreline fertilized with seaweed is an ideal place for the sea kale to grow. Sea kale is used as vegetable, but only the very young leaf stems are edible.

The loosestrife, with its crimson colour, towers over most of the other vegetations on the beaches, and seems to thrive very well in the mild coastal climate of Sørlandet. Historically the plant has been used to treat typhoid fever and as a medicine against diarrhoea.

The asteraceae grows well both on pebble beaches and in small cracks in the rocks. There, it grows in salty soil and seems completely unaffected by the whipping wind and the constant shower of seawater.

Dog rose

Loosestrife

Bloody cranesbill

Sea kale

Asteraceae

Caprifole

Butterflies

The favourable climate along the Southern Coast, the good nutritional conditions, and the long growing season are the reasons why we find a number of plants that normally grow in more southerly latitudes. Barberries, dog rose, caprifole, black berries and black thorn are plants that thrive in warm climates. The insects appreciate that, for the flora is not the only interesting element along the coast, the insect fauna is also extremely diverse and multifaceted. For example, in the Tromøy part of the moraine, 1372 types of butterfly have been registered – the highest number of butterflies registered in any area in Norway.

Apollo butterfly

It is no coincidence that precisely this area is so thoroughly mapped. The well known entomologist, Alf Bakke, has for years had a summer place in Bjelland at Tromøy. Together with eager assistants, he has allowed the lamps to burn all through the summer nights and registered new butterfly species.

The plants we find growing on the shore are particularly important for the insect life. Garden angelica and valerianaceae are among the favourites of the beautiful swallowtail, which is normally found along the whole coast of Norway, just before summer, from end of May to beginning of July.

The importance of beach vegetation for the insects is easy to understand when we know that the blackthorn is a host plant for fifteen different butterflies.

However, the butterfly fauna has changed. Until the 1960s, the beautiful Apollo butterfly was very common on the Southern Coast. Then something inexplicable happened. In the course of a decade, the butterfly disappeared from the coastal landscape. An Apollo butterfly along the Southern Coast will almost be a sensation today.

Swallowtail carterpillar on a garden angelica

Swallowtail

A compass rose carved in stone – from the sailing ship era.

In the Footsteps of Our Ancestors

The First Southerners

Ever since the great glaciers retreated and left behind a small strip of dry land way out on the coast, people have lived on the Southern Coast of Norway. About ten thousand years ago, the first hunters paddled in their primitive boats across the sea, and from the moment they set foot on land they left traces behind.

We find traces of Stone Age people on the coast from Kristiansand to Lista. When bits of skeleton were found in a shallow bay in Hummervikholmen in Søgne, it created much attention. C-14 dating showed that the remains were 8600 years old, and that the oldest skeleton find in Norway belonged to at least two women.

One of the most famous places in Lista area is Penne and its vicinity. Here you find clear rock carvings of ships, bowl hollows and "footprints." One reckons that they were made about three thousand years ago. In the same area, there are ancient ruins left behind from the settlers' dwellings, burial mounds from the Iron Age and stone fences both from older and more recent times.

Stone carvings in Lista

THE ROCK CARVINGS AT PENNE IN LISTA ARE ABOUT 3000 YEARS OLD, AND SHOW THE IMPORTANCE OF BOATS BOTH IN THE DAILY LIFE AND AFTER DEATH.

The grave mounds at the islands Tromlingene and Jerken by Arendal are relics with high national priority. One reckons that the graves can be from 1800 - 1000 B.C. There are numerous grave mounds in the archipelago of Grimstad and Lillesand.

The Bronze Age people usually buried their dead under monumental mounds on heights. The dead had to see and be seen. Therefore, the view of the sea and the paths and roads decided the location of the mounds.

The burial mounds were raised over the graves of the most powerful people in the region. The coffin itself, built of stone, was usually laid directly on the rocks in the middle of the mound. All burial mounds have long been plundered and the gifts stolen.

The famous Bronze Age sword from Møglestu in Lillesand, and the so-called "face urns" from Vik at Grimstad, show that Bronze Age people had close contact with the continent.

For the time being, Spangereid, the canal across the low isthmus, is unique in Norway, and has very few parallels in Scandinavia. The three hundred meters long manmade canal has connected the natural harbour at Kjerkevågen with the waters within Spangereid, enabling vessels to travel from the harbour westwards without having to cross the dangerous sea around Lindesnes. The original canal stems probably from the first migrations.

Medieval church in Tromøya

Burial mound at Tromlingene on Tromøya outside Arendal

The Era of Sailing Ships

In Sørlandet, there has always been good communication between those living in the fjords and those living furthest out towards the open sea. The fishermen seldom had to go far to exchange goods. They traded halibut with meat, butter and baste rope, on the church hill after the Sunday sermon.

What we call the true sailing ship era lasted from about 1850 to WWI. Of course, there were ships and sailors long before that, but during this period the fleet expanded considerably, providing jobs for a large number of people along the Southern Coast.

The islands furthest out at sea and along the ship route were clustered with white and red houses. These were the homes of the fishermen, the sailors, and the harbour pilots. White houses with tiled roofs were signs of wealth. Shipping created activity and affluence in the outer harbours, because they were safe havens for ships seeking a port of refuge due to storm or illness.

An epidemic on board required that the ship be quarantined in the vicinity of the coastal pilot's and customs' offices. The dead were brought back to land and buried in the 'cholera churchyards' in the archipelago.

The ships that moored in an outer harbour had to pay a fee. Many places there were huge rings or T-poles in the rocks. A few well placed rings could secure a handsome annual income.

Poles were used to kedge the sailing ships out of the harbour when the wind was calm.

A bottle ship, built by Kjell Birkeland, Arendal.
In Arendal you can find an impressive collection of bottle-ships in the City library.

Ballast Plants

A signpost with two spades crossing each other were one of the most common symbols for ballast along the coast. It showed where it was allowed to dump the ballast-soil and stones taken on board to stabilize the ship without cargo. In this soil there were often planting seeds. When the seeds sprouted, both flowers and weeds spread in the southern archipelago. We call these imported plants ballast plants.

Along the Southern Coast, we find a number of plants brought back with ship from other countries. They are called ballast plants, and two hundred are registered in Norway. Many are considered weeds, but some are beautiful flowers. The wild tulip and the Kenilworth ivy are good examples, which are now the municipality flowers of Arendal and Tvedestrand respectively.

Most ships freighted timber abroad, but they seldom brought anything back. To sail without cargo was a game of chance, because the heavy weight of the rig and sails made the ships dependent on cargo, or a ballast, to maintain stability at sea. Therefore, they had ballast on board the ships when they had to return without cargo. On arrival to Sørlandet, the ballast was unloaded – often straight into the sea.

Sometimes the skippers wanted to bring back good soil for their gardens in the outer harbour. In this ballast soil there were many types of seeds. The skippers probably never thought about that, because in addition to the soil, they often brought along beautiful garden plants to have in their gardens. Later some of these spread in the nature. Goutweed, which was originally brought back as a medicinal plant, is now considered a weed.

Pineappleweed is one of the few plants we know with reasonable certainty when it came to Norway. It is said to have been in the soil on board a ship that came to Arendal in 1881. The seeds from the pineappleweed spread quickly, because they clung to shoes and wagon wheels. Therefore, in the course of a few years the plant had spread all over Norway.

Other typical ballast plants are the low mallow, radium weed, black medick, creeping cinquefoil, scarlet pimpernel, broadweed, pepperweed, lesser swinecress, sand leek, quickweed and matrem.

Kenilworth ivy

Ballast sign

Wild tulip

The Coastal Birds

The Gulls

During summer, many of these species nest at the mouth of the archipelago where they lay their eggs, watch over them and feed their chicks. The need for food is obviously enormous in this period.

Notice what happens when you clean the fish on the way back from your fishing trip. In just a few moments, the gulls are all over the boat and fight relentlessly over each and every morsel. There are obvious hierarchies in the stocks. When the oldest gulls arrive, the others make way immediately.

The gulls can be both sociable and trusting. If you fish in the same place a few days in a row and treat the gulls in a friendly manner, you will soon find a gull sitting on the steering – loyal like an old friend. The eyes, though, speak out clearly: “You got an extra piece of fish?”

Earlier, most gulls were usually seen in the harbours. Since many of the fish halls have closed down, the gulls have been forced to go somewhere else to find food.

The herring gull looks like a large common gull, but it has pink legs and a distinct red spot on its bill. You will find gulls just as well in a landfill as in the outer reaches of the archipelago.

THE SEAGULLS ARE THE SOVEREIGN COASTAL BIRDS OF SØRLANDET

Why Do They Always Screech?

For most of us the screeching of the gulls gives pleasant associations to sun, summer, swimming and warmth. The seagull screeches are downright pleasant sounds that tell us that summer's here and it's time for holidays! We are in high spirits until we move just a few meters away from our delicious picnic lunch. The seagulls are there immediately. The food suddenly vanishes and you curse the seagull rabble.

Some say that seagulls don't screech – they talk to each other. What we humans experience as a racket on a fine summer day is the birds' communication with each other. This has many important functions. First of all, the gulls screech in order to attract the attention of their 'friends', or other birds or animals. That birdsong is used to attract mates, defend a territory or warn family and friends is a well known fact. But that it can also be actively used in order to create contact between adult birds and their young is not so well known. Rather sympathetic really, if you think about it.

If you have the chance, sit near a colony of gulls where the adult birds and their chicks are gathered together. You will discover a variety of sounds. The intensity and rhythm of the sounds change from tender to exceptionally aggressive, when the birds feel threatened or are fighting over food.

The greater black back is the largest of the gulls along our coast. It is an omnivorous bird of prey.

The common gull, or the mew gull, as its name indicates is the most common sort of gulls. It can be found all over the country – even by inland freshwater and by the mountain lakes. The common gull has yellow green bill and legs.

The lesser black-backed gull (on the left) has black back and the wings are also black on the top. It looks like a black-back but it is smaller and has yellow feet.

The black-headed gull (on the right) is easily recognizable – at least in spring and summer. Because then it has a chocolate brown hood. During winter the hood is reduced to a grey spot behind the eyes.

Eurasian Oystercatcher and Tern

The Eurasian oystercatcher with its red legs is very common along the Southern Coast. It is easy to detect when it treads lightly in the shallow water looking for mussels. Quickly, it hacks the mussel to pieces with its powerful chisel-like, reddish-orange bill. This particular wader has remarkable ability to crack and eat scores of shells in a short time. It is not unusual to see one bird manage to pick and open several hundred shells in the course of a day.

There are about forty thousand Eurasian oystercatchers in Norway. They are migratory birds, and the migration in autumn begins already in August. The majority of the birds spend the winter in England, Germany and the Netherlands.

Few signs of spring are more welcome than the arrival of the Eurasian oystercatchers in March. The first days after their return, they sit quietly at the tip of the reef and rest after their long journey across the North Sea. But then they resume their life, flying across the archipelago with vigorous short flaps of their wings. The oystercatchers can become very old. The oldest we know of is over thirty years.

The tern is temperamental. It won't take long from when you land on an islet where the tern has a nest or chicks, before you realize you have done something stupid – something very stupid! The thing to do is turn around fast, because this hothead never gives up. You can risk being hacked bloody if you don't retreat immediately.

At first glance, the tern seems like a peaceful and gracious bird flying systematically along the coast in search of its next meal-the same route back and forth. It hunts patiently, calmly and with concentration until it suddenly locates the prey, and elegantly dives into the water and resurfaces with the catch in its beak.

For many people the arrival of the terns in spring finally heralds the onset of summer. On their arrival in Norway, the terns have flown all the way from the coast of Southern and Western Africa. The first days after their arrival they are very quiet. It seems like they need to rest after their journey, but then suddenly their characteristic sounds are heard all over the Archipelago. And what a wonderful sound it is!

Eurasian oystercatcher

Tern

The Common Eider

The common eider is the coast's most ordinary duck. Although it can be seen both in the Southern Coast and at Svalbard, it is in the coastal areas north of Trøndelag and particularly on the Helgeland coast that the largest stocks gather. In these areas, eggs and eiderdown have been traded since the times of the Vikings. In northern Norway, the eider was a 'domestic animal' for several hundred years, providing both egg and down. In southern Norway, we do not have the same tradition. Here, we have been mostly concerned with the question wheter they eat the small lobsters.

The eider eats many different sorts of shellfish, such as mussels, sea urchins and sea porcupines but that it eats small lobsters must be an old superstition. There is no scientific evidence for that claim. If you still have doubts, we can reveal that analyses of the contents of the eiders' stomachs show that their favourite food is not lobster, but small mussels which the bird swallows whole. The gizzard, the powerful grinding stomach of the bird, grinds the shells.

Because the stock is large in the Southern Coast, the hunting season is now between October 1 and December 1.

The female lays four to six eggs in April -May, in a nest padded with the finest down. She incubates day and night for four weeks, almost without leaving the nest. During this period the female bird loses one third of her body weight.

If the brooding eider is frightened, she covers the eggs with down before leaving the nest. That way the eggs are less visible to gulls and other notorious egg snatchers. If she has to flee quickly, she defecates on the eggs. There are strong indications that the bird excrement keeps the egg snatchers away.

The eider ducks are good divers and can easily dive down to thirty meters depth. When the eider swims, it looks like it is almost "flying" through the water with fast flapping wings.

Eider (female) nesting

Egg and eiderdown

A male eider (to the right)

Greylag and other Geese

The greylags' numbers have increased dramatically in the last fifteen to twenty years. Earlier, it nested almost only on the Rogaland coast to Porsanger fjord in Finnmark. The past few years, it has also settled down along the southern coast.

The ornithologists believe that the reason for the positive development is that in the 60s many birds were set out in the Oslo Fjord. The increasing stocks have made the greylag a favourite with the hunters along larger parts of the coast. In some areas, the flocks have become a problem for the farmers.

The greylag is extremely shy. It is therefore difficult to estimate the number of nests in Norway, but we believe that there are approximately seven to ten thousand pairs. This comprises a large part of the Northern European stock.

Our greylags are different from the middle European geese in that they nest on islets and islands along the coast and not in freshwater or brackish water. Norwegian greylags graze also mainly on grass and herbs, while other greylags mostly graze on water plants.

Tagging results have shown that the greylags spend winter in Spain and the Netherlands. Earlier the greylags migrated to the south during September. The migration schedule has undergone marked changes during the last five to ten years, probably because of the increasing pressure from hunting. The geese from mid Norway migrate before the hunting season begins.

The barnacle goose now nests in Sørlandet. In 1986, a pair of nesting barnacle geese was observed at the island Stråholmen in Telemark. This couple was probably the pioneers that initiated the spread of the stock from the Baltic Sea to the North West. A stock that later resulted in a solid settlement in the Gothenburg archipelago.

The first incubation in Aust-Agder County was observed in 2000, in Tvedestrand. The same year, they were seen nesting in Østfold County.

The largest nesting barnacle geese today are on the east coast of Greenland, in Svalbard and north of Russia.

Around 1970, Edvin K. Thorson set out forty barnacle goslings from the Russian stock in the Ekeberg Park, in Oslo.

In 1979, a couple of barnacle geese settled down at Malmøya, deep within the Oslofjord, to incubate. The stock of barnacle geese has since gradually increased, and the last count from 2001 showed seventy-three birds.

Barnacle goose

Greylag

The Cormorants Invade the Southern Coast

We have around thirty types of cormorants in the world, three of these are found in Europe. The great cormorant is the most common. The sinensis cormorant has had en explosive development during these last thirty to forty years in North-West Europe. Now the number is also increasing along the southern coast of Norway.

Undoubtedly, the cormorant is far more common in the Sørlandet now than twenty years ago. The extensive establishment of nesting places in the last years indicate that the bird is here to stay.

In North-West Europe, the flock has been growing from 3500 pairs in the beginning of the 60s, to well over a hundred thousand pairs, in 2003. The majority of the cormorants are found in Poland, Germany, The Netherlands, Denmark and Sweden. In these countries, the cormorants' enormous fish consumption has enraged both the coastal fishermen and the hobby fishers, and actions have been taken to reduce their numbers.

During the last years, several studies have been undertaken to prove that the cormorants eat considerable amounts of fish. 'Considerable' means approximately 300 grams of fish per day. Their diet varies both with season and habitat, but a variety of shore fish are always an important part of the cormorants' diet.

The smaller wrasses: yellow green, and goldsinny wrasse, together with Canestrini's kutling, small cod and eel make up the cormorants' main diet.

New calculations, based on Swedish surveys, show that the cormorant stock of about four thousand birds in Hvaler catch the same amount of cod in Østfold as the coastal fishermen do.

From October 1 to December 1, it is hunting season for year old cormorants in Sørlandet. The chicks are distinguishable by their light coloured breasts.

Hunting cormorants is demanding. Best results are achieved by using a decoy placed on top of isles and rocks in the cormorants' migration route. The silhouettes of cormorants in characteristic positions are cut in wood and painted black. The hunter must set out at dawn, on days with off-shore wind, and sit still and quiet as the birds approach the decoy and come into close range. Cormorants are tough birds to shoot. Therefore, it is necessary to use large pellets (nr. 3 or bigger). Traditionally, one uses long barrelled rifles specially made for cormorant hunting.

It is a common misconception that the meat tastes of fish oil. It does not taste of fish oil, but it does taste like seabird. Just like with whale meat, it is difficult to avoid a faint taste of marine fatty acids when you eat seabirds. A good tip is to remove the fat from the breast filet, pack it in a couple of pieces of smoked ham and fry it like a steak. We can guarantee a fantastic culinary experience.

On the Southern Coast, the cormorants hatch in peace and the stock is growing.
In some parts of Denmark, they have attempted to control the stock by, among other things, to spray oil on the eggs.

Hunting cormorants in autumn is exciting.

Heron

Heron is the only type of stork that nests in Norway. In the South Coast, during the last few years, the grey heron has increased in number.

The grey heron's wingspan is nearly two meters. The long legged bird is impossible to confuse with any other bird along the coast. But the heron is a shy bird which is difficult to approach. It is both majestic and clumsy when it is frightened and takes flight. Its head and neck are not quite "together" in the beginning. After a while, they fall in place and the heron acquires its well known flying style with its long neck pulled back into an S-form.

The heron has very sharp eyes and is an expert at getting close to its prey. Its strategy is simple but effective. It stands like a meter long wooden stick in the shallow water, completely still, for hours, and waits for a suitable prey to come by. When a small fish is close enough, the heron quickly plunges and snaps it up with its dagger bill.

The grey heron is spread over large parts of Europe, Asia and Africa. Although widespread across Norway, it is mostly concentrated along the coast.

The herons like to live in colonies. They build large twig nests in trees, or on cliffs or steep hillsides. They lay eggs early – already in March. The eggs are blue, but almost like chicken eggs in shape and size.

After four weeks of incubation, three to five chicks hatch. They are demanding and remain in the nest for almost two months. During this time, one can therefore hear a huge racket from the screeching chicks in the heron colony. Both the sound and the smell reveal the nesting places, because close to the nesting areas the stench of rotting fish is often overwhelming.

The heron must have easy access to shallow beaches with abundant fish, because although it also eats frogs, mice and snails, fish is its main staple. It eats mainly small wrasses, small seaweed fishes and fry. The grey heron manages to catch small coalfish, and other pelagic fish. Once in a while, it aims at larger fish, but only manages to wound them because it is unable to lift them up.

Most grey herons spend the winter along the coast. On stormy days, they stand with their backs to the wind and their "shoulders" raised around their head. They can stand in this position for hours. If the winter is long and cold and the birds have a hard time finding a snug and safe place away from the wind and weather, many young birds die. Their feathers are thin and do not provide enough protection against the cold.

The grey heron stock is growing rapidly in number all over Norway. Not everyone is pleased with this progress, because the heron helps itself to the juvenile trout fry in the coastal waterways. In western Norway, it has become extremely unpopular because it is attracted to the fish farms where it can pick and choose its meal.

Two-spotted goby

Heron "fishing" in the low tide

The Swans

Most people like swans – at least from a distance. The reason for our warm feelings towards swans may be the fairytale *The Ugly Duckling*. But to be honest, they are not particularly charming neighbours to have on the beach. They often behave aggressively, and leave huge blobs of excrement on the beaches.

On the Southern Coast, there are both whooper swans and mute swans, but the latter are the most common. They began to settle down as late as in 1973. Now there are 1500 pairs, and they take space.

The easiest way to see the difference between mute swans and whooper swans is the black knob of skin at the base of their bills, and the throbbing of their wings when they fly. The whooper swans lack both the knob and the wing throbbing. They prefer the shallow parts of the archipelago, particularly areas with brackish water, where they graze the water plants and catch small marine animals. The common eelgrass seems to be the whooper swans' favourite food. But during summer they seek out the beaches in order to beg for goodies from the bathers.

The mute swans only eat water plants and build their nests on the edge of the water in a cove or on an islet. The birds share the incubating work. The grey cygnets swim together with their parents just after hatching until the end of autumn.

The mute swans remain all winter in the South Coast, if they can find ice free areas – and they often do.

The Swans are large, heavy animals, nevertheless they are good flyers. A few years ago, English biologists attached radio senders on a few whooper swans, and registered that the birds flew from Iceland to Britain, a distance of 1200 km, only in nine hours. Airplane pilots have reported seeing whooper swans at several thousand meters height.

A swan couple in Sandøykilen

Sea Eagle in Sørlandet!

The sea eagle is Northern Europe's largest bird of prey. With its two and a half meters wingspan, powerful beak and sharp claws, it is an awesome sight. It has recently been observed nesting in some parts of the Southern Coast.

The preservation of the sea eagle has been one of our greatest nature conservation successes. After it became preserved in 1968, the stock has increased tremendously. From the central areas on the Helgeland Coast, the sea eagle has settled further south and has now become quite common in the western part of Norway. In Vest-Agder, the sea eagle was observed nesting for the first time in 2005.

Earlier, we were overjoyed to see one or two sea eagles soaring high up in the sky a couple of times a year.

The sea eagle is one of four Norwegian bird species that are on the international 'red list' of globally endangered birds.

Norway has a particularly great responsibility for the species, because we have such a large stock in our country. There are an estimated two thousand nesting couples in Norway.

The sea eagle's wings are long, broad and rectangular. The tail is short and triangular. Old birds are recognizable by their white tails.

The peregrine falcon – "the coastal fighter plane." – flying high up in the sky, it scouts with hawk eyes in search of its next meal. The attack on the unsuspecting prey comes literally like "lightning out of a clear sky." The peregrine falcon's stoop, the hunting dive, is legendary. With its great precision and a speed over 100 km/h, the peregrine falcon is a fantastically effective hunter.

The pelegrin falcon often resides in areas with many birds – close to bird cliffs or wetlands along the whole coastal area.

Wild and beautiful

From being an endangered species, the peregrine falcon has spread all along the Southern Coast. During a period in the 70s, the number of peregrine falcons fell to a critical level. The use of dangerous environmental poisons, particularly the insecticide DDT, had dramatic consequences for the birds, because the poison reduced their reproduction ability and the egg-shells became too thin to tolerate incubation. Today, the stock is growing and no longer endangered.

Sea Eagle

Peregrine Falcon

TO EXPERIENCE AN ALMOST UNINTERRUPTED STRETCH OF NATURE RESERVE FOR OUTDOOR RECREATION ALL YEAR ROUND, HEAD FOR THE COAST OF TELEMARK AND THE TWIN COUNTIES OF AGDER

The Norwegian Riviera

Sørlandet

Sørlandet has much to offer both visitors and locals – during all seasons of the year. In the London newspaper *The Independent,* journalist Siobhan Mulholland, in 2002 wrote an article about her summer experiences on what she called "The Norwegian Riviera".

She pointed out that Norway is officially the best place in the world to live, according to the UN, and she personnally recommended the coastline as outstanding for a holiday.

Norway's peaceful southern coast

The term "Riviera" conjures up images of a society playground with flashy yachts and bragging wealth. Of course you can find expencive yachts and summerhouses along the coast, but this is not what you should expected to find along the Skagerrak Coast – although this coastline is Norwegians' favourite summer destination.

We invite you to explore the peaceful south-eastern coastline from Langesund down to Lindesnes, and even further west to Flekkefjord. Scenically it is stunning: mile upon mile of tiny rocky islands and skerries, hidden bays and coves, tempting sandy beaches, white traditional houses and clear glistening fjords. The archipelago of Sørlandet is spacious – here is room for everyone.

www.visitsorlandet.com

LANGESUND

Langøya and Langøytangen lighthouse are worth a visit. Located close to the town centre, the nature reserve has attractive flora, fine beaches and great fishing spots.

The lighthouse on Langøytangen towers majestically. It is currently used by the Langesund Fjord Coast Club, as part of the Coastal Route, Kystleden.

Langesund is a charming, distinctive and hospitable town in the northeast end of the Coastal Archipelago Park. Langesund is the community centre of Bamble municipality. The sea and shipping have been important parts of its history. Tordenskiold's flag ship, *Løvendahl's Galley*, was built here in 1712.

Nowadays, Langesund is more a summer resort rather than a shipping town. Already for more than a hundred years ago, Langesund had a reputation as a summer resort. The Langesund bath is history, but it has been replaced by the Skjærgården Hotel and resort, in tune with the changing trends. It is conveniently located at a strolling distance from the guest harbour.

Kongshavn is a historical harbour used by the Viking chiefs. Håkon Håkonson himself used this harbour, when he sailed from Bjørgvin (now Bergen) to Tunsberg in 1240.

The most resplendent and grand building in Langesund is the old Town Hall. It was originally built as a residence in 1785, but was bought by the municipality in 1862.

The culture house, Wrigthegaarden, is also a listed building from the eighteenth century. Today, it comprises an art gallery, a restaurant, a pub and a charming garden-perhaps best known for its concerts, with famous national and international artists on the programme.

Langesund Fishing Festival is one of the largest sea fishing competitions in Norway. The competition has many entry classes, such as catching as many different sorts of fish as possible, in the course of two days.

There is a wide variety of fish species just off Langesund. Fifty sorts of fish have been caught during the years the festival has existed, but there are presumably more than seventy different species in the sea outside Langesund.

The fishing takes place at all depths from two to four hundred and fifty meters. And they all give results. It is possible to catch big fish, such as ling and cod, close to shore, because the Langesund fjord reaches a depth of two hundred metres, even all the way inside the fjord.

Since so many records have been set in the

Langesund Fishing Festival is arranged by Bamble Hunting and Fishing Association and takes place on the second weekend of August. During the festival, the town is seething with life, and you can experience fishing competitions for children, concerts and a taste of the delicacies from the sea prepared by master chefs.

Langesund bay, there is a great interest from foreigners to come to Langesund to try their luck off the fishing boat *JERA*, which is owned by Grefstad Havfiske. The good chances of catching large lings, cusk, and pale rays tempt the enthusiasts among the sea fishers.

Of course, all have the opportunity to try their fishing luck. If you are a "land crab," talk with the locals if you want to fish from your own boat, or contact the tourist information or local fishermen for a sea fishing tour.

Catchfly

The Coast of Bamble

The coast of Bamble is a paradise for boat tourists. The long coastline has a varied archipelago with countless possibilities. Indeed, the area has so many wonderful places that you can easily spend a long time there and still find a new fine harbour each day without any problem.

When heading southwest, we suggest that you keep to the signposted and protected waterway, Tonerleia, on the inner side of Såstein. Såstein is one of the wonderful islands of the Bamble Archipelago, and has fantastic polished rocks, many mooring rings and several spots for fishing and bathing. Part of the island is a bird sanctuary.

Åbyfjorden is the small arm of the fjord in the west, straight out from Langesund on the way to Tonerleia. It is an attractive fjord with many islets and little islands with fine harbours, for example the old ship harbour Elvik, or the small inlets Valvik and Hyvik.

Within the fjord, at the mouth of the river Åby-elva, you will find Arneplass, where the children can set off on expeditions up the river in true "Indiana Jones" style. Kråka, southwest of Brevikstrand, also belongs to the Coastal Archipelago Park and is well organised for boaters. The island is a very popular place for outings, but since there are many underwater stones and sand mounds, you need to take it slowly and keep a good view from the bow.

The characteristic Tonerkollen in Tonerhavn was the lookout point for the harbour pilots. Although somewhat small, Tonerhavn provides a safe shelter, protected against wind from any direction.
Valle marina is considered by many as Sørlandet's best service and shopping centre. It has twenty five guest places and "all" facilities. If you find it too urbanized, head for the archipelago's peace and quiet a little further out in the fjord.
Continuing southwest, through Klokkersund en route for Store Skrue, you will come to Stråholmen in the southeast.

If you want to go to Kragerø, we recommend the route through Kreppa. It is narrow, but the water is clean. Keep going straight ahead through Skjensundet north of Berøy. Kragerø will be directly in front.

Fine natural harbours and great bathing spots

The skerries outside Havsund are fantastic and within the fjord there are cosy inlets, fine bathing spots and safe mooring places for both large and small vessels.

Havsund is the entrance to Trosbyfjorden, with a marina and good facilities. Inside Trosbyfjorden there are snug inlets for mooring or anchoring. Rødlandet in Trosbyfjorden is part of the Coastal Archipelago Park, and is specially prepared for boaters and visitors by car. There you have a small boat harbour, rocks, grass and sandy beaches. The water is shallow in that area, perfect for families with small children.

The Archipelago of Bamble
There are clusters of islands at the mouth of the fjord, and you will find other sheltered inlets within the archipelago. Despite the many cottages and summer houses in the area, it is easy to find your "own" little beach where both grownups and children can enjoy themselves, bathing and fishing.

The islands Jomfruland and Stråholmen are located out at sea.

Stråholmen

Stråholmen

The island Stråholmen is located way out at sea, north of Jomfruland and south of Tonerleia. From a distance, Stråholmen seems neither large nor resplendent, but gradually one discovers a gorgeous island – a true gem in the midst of the sea.

To go ashore on Stråholmen is like taking a few steps back in time. The houses are built in areas protected from the weather and show that this has been a prosperous community. People have been living here since the seventeenth century. The building methods witness a close contact with the continent.

The idyllic houses are built close to each other for mutual protection against the autumn and winter storms. At its height, Stråholmen had forty-nine residents. They got by with what the sea and the land provided, but in 1954 the last resident left the island. Since then, the houses have been used as summer places and cottages.

Stråholmen was one of the country's first pilot harbours. For a while during the nineteenth century, there were three pilots working there. The pilotage generated good income, because the boat traffic through the tricky waters to Kragerø was busy. In winter, it was among the most dangerous waterways, and during the sailing ship era there were many shipwrecks.

Although there are a number of houses and cottages in Stråholmen, you are welcome to visit. Here you can find a nice beach and a small football field for the children, a pier and a fantastic nature. Watch out for the hidden rocks and shallow areas when you sail into the harbour. There are two ways in to Stråholmen. The safest is from the north.

For most of the year, both animals and plants are left in peace. Stråholmen's nature reserve and protected wetland areas have the most diverse bird species in Telemark. The seashore is internationally recognized as important to protect. Like Jomfruland, Stråholmen is among the places where the spring birds arrive first, either to rest before continuing their long journey, or to settle down in the vicinity. The ornithologists monitor the bird life on the island, which has resulted in many interesting observations in the area.

Earlier, Stråholmen had almost no vegetation, but today it is becoming more overgrown each year. The reason is the lack of farming and grazing animals on the island. To prevent overgrowth, the municipality has placed out a few hardy Norwegian sheep.

In the recent years, flocks of seals have been observed on the small islets and bedrocks.

Jomfruland

Jomfruland is one of the most attractive places on the coast line of Sørlandet. It does not resemble any of the other islands along that coast. The island is covered with flat fields and dense woods, with pebble beaches on the outer side and sandy beaches on the inner side. The pastures are fenced in with characteristic stone and pole fences. In spring, the ground in the woods is carpeted with wood anemones.

Jomfruland is seven kilometres long and about one kilometre wide in most parts. Along the outer part, the pebble beaches stretch almost all the length of the island, acting as wave breakers against the Skagerrak. Øytangen on the north-eastern part of the island has the finest sandy beach in all the Kragerø Coastline.

Jomfruland is a flat moraine with lush vegetation, and is the most famous island in the Kragerø archipelago. Like a mini Denmark, it is located in its characteristic manner in the middle of the sea with meadows, cows, deciduous forests, gravel paths, sandy beaches and pebbles.

Take time to experience the nature, the flowers and the scent, the bird song, and the idyllic paths, perfect for cycling and walks.

From early spring, the ferries provide a shuttle service between Kragerø and Jomfruland. The island is particularly attractive when the anemones are in bloom, but it has qualities in all seasons – as increasingly more people are discovering.

Two lighthouses rise in the middle of the green forest. The lighthouses, with their protruding tops are a familiar and cherished landmark for all sailors. The view from the lighthouse is fantastic. You can see far and wide across Skagerrak and the skerries outside Kragerø.

The oldest lighthouse was built in 1838, and was operative the year after. In the lighthouse there is also a small museum with a collection of equipments for operating a lighthouse. In the lighthouse manager's building, there is a natural history exhibition, where art exhibitions are sometimes arranged.

Painters have always been inspired by the nature in Jomfruland. The most famous picture from Jomfruland is probably painted by Theodor Kittelsen. Not many people know that he used Tårntjernet as model for his famous fairy tale drawing *Nøkken*.

The guest harbour in Jomfruland is not so big, and the boat places at Tårnbrygga usually fill up quickly. Boats queuing up to wait for a vacant place are a common sight. If you have the possibility, you can moor to a buoy in the bay outside the small boat harbour. If you want to sleep safely, it is advisable to find a place within the quay, because north easterly winds can make the sea unpleasantly rough outside the wave breakers.

The taxi boats "own" the waterways on the inner side of Jomfruland. They are a visible sign of the urbanization that marks this part of the Southern Coast. The increasing numbers of summer cottages and guests, Jomfruland's popularity as a resort and the summer attractions in Kragerø, have their price. Those who loaf around between islands in a little boat have to be on the watch all the time, ready to give way. It's no use to stand up for your rights. The taxi boats have a job to do, and no time to lose.

Jomfruland's two lighthouses

Tårntjernet

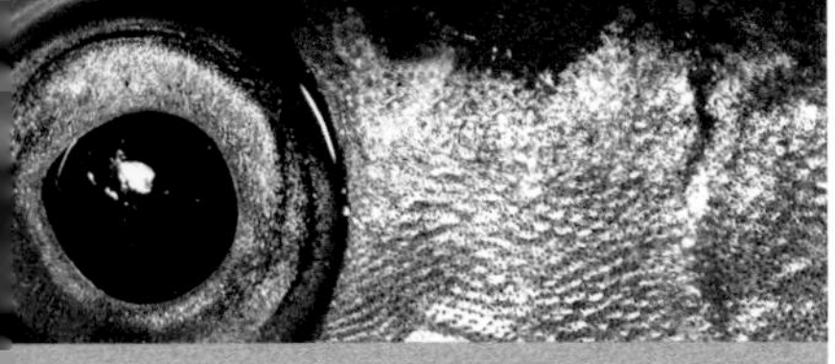

Within Jomfruland

According to the Norwegian artist, Christian Krohg, this is the most beautiful archipelago in Norway. The area is gorgeous. You have to search far and wide to find a place that can match the Archipelago of Jomfruland.

The nature is varied and consists of great natural beauties such as the islands Skåtøy, Arøy, Gumøy, Berøy and Langøy, and also many inhabited and uninhabited islets and bedrocks. Not surprisingly, the area has more than three thousand cottages, summer houses and a one kilometre long dock for visitors. Nevertheless, it is often hard to find vacant places. There are cottages almost everywhere. If the Kragerø archipelago had not been so vast, it would have been a big problem. The 495 islands luckily include also eighty-four recreation areas, consisting of 1750 acres of nature reserve and public access to the archipelago, with many fine places for mooring the boat, camping and bathing.

Right within Jomfruland, northeast of Skåtøy, you find Jesperholmane and Schweigårdsholmen with beautiful rocks and great bathing spots. Vestre Rauane is also a popular destination in good weather. This fantastic, small cluster of islands with polished rocks is located at the outermost end of the archipelago, towards Skagerrak. The way in from the west is easy if a little narrow. The lagoon within is sheltered against the wind. It is often difficult to find mooring places during the summer holidays, but June and August are quiet months.

If you venture further out to sea, you can find cosy places for coffee breaks and bathing.

Southwest of Strømtangen is Fengsholmen, with a good fair-weather harbour with mooring bolts and fine camping sites.

There are also camping sites on Dypsundsholmene, in the middle of Kilsfjorden southwest of Tåtøy. Some islets are private, but the rest are part of the Nature Reserve of the Archipelago. There are many fine bathing spots and small sandy beaches.

Jomfruland
The view from Jomfruland Lighthouse reveals that the surrounding waters are sprinkled with big and small islets, many with summer-houses and cottages. The areas off Jomfruland to the west have the best beaches.

Saltneven – Kragerø Sailing Club – is a little islet west of Skåtøy. Here you can see the traditional sailing boats "Krageøterner." These sailing boats are the results of a competition, in 1938, to develop an ideal sailing vessel for children. For many years, this boat class was the biggest in the Sørlandet Regatta.

The ferry service to the large islands is good, and few coastal towns have a better taxi boat service than Kragerø.

Skrata
Between Skåtøy and Jomfruland you find Skrata with its wide and flat rocks and cosy inlets and small rounded fjords. The island is well organised for boat tourists.

Båtøybukta
on the east side of Skåtøy is a good natural harbour, well protected from the southerly and westerly winds.

Korset
On the inner side of Østre Rauene you will find a fine, inviting harbour.

The view from the Jomfruland Lighthouse

It's good to sit on the pier along "Blindtarmen" with a cold drink.
During the summer holidays, you can go almost dryshod across the small harbour,
which many people call Kragerø's Venice.

KRAGERØ

Kragerø lies well protected within the idyllic and wide-ranging archipelago. Sailing in is an experience in itself, and if you come by car you should treat yourself to a taxi boat trip through the archipelago- and visit Jomfruland for example.

Kragerø became a trading town in 1666. Large parts of the old buildings burnt down in the great fire in 1711, but along Barthebrygga and on Øya there are several well-preserved manor houses that survived the fire.

Biørnegården, Kragerø's town hall, was designed by Emil Victor Langslet, who also drew the Storting in Oslo.

Gunnarsholmen is a popular place to visit. The splendid park with the open-air swimming pool is very popular both for tourists and residents. You will not find a better "public bath" anywhere else along the coast. But the rest of Gunnarsholmen is also interesting with its splendid canons. From being a citizen battery run by volunteer home guards in the nineteenth century, they are now used as salute canons in formal ceremonies.

Kragerø has undoubtedly its own characteristic charm, located cosily behind Øya. The main streets along the sea are particularly charming, with cafés and small pleasant shops.

"Kragerø has a bustling, funfair feel to it during summer. The winding streets are so delightfully unregulated, unsuitable for cars but perfect for pedestrians."
(Odd Børretzen)

Art lovers have much to look forward to, because during summer the town's cultural activities are blooming. Visit one of the many small galleries. Theodor Kittilsen Museum is fun also for children.

The open-air swimming pool at Gunnarsholmen

Portør

For a long time Portør was one of the most important outports along the coast. In contrast to many of the other known outports along the Southern Coast, Portør is part of the mainland, located way out on the Levang peninsula, and can be reached by car. The place is therefore among the most popular holiday destination in Kragerø.

There are many bathing spots in Portør, and there is a network of paths leading to fine fishing places, if you like fishing from shore.

Portør was originally one the most important customs and pilot harbours along the Skagerrak Coast. But the harbour was known already during the Viking era. The sagas recount that ships gathered in this harbour before beginning their raids. Sigurd Slembe lay in wait with his fleet in Portør in 1137, to take ships that sailed past. Also King Sverre used the harbour, so did his enemies and the Danish king, Valdemar. In other words, Portør has historical aura.

Nowadays, the boaters are primarily attracted to the polished rocks and all the sheltered natural harbours. There are many good places to moor along the islets off Portør (see maps on page 180 and 186). By Uerholmene there is a beautiful lagoon, and around Dapholmene there are many nice places. It is tempting to head towards Flatskjær on fine days. In Portør there are hotels, boarding houses and cafés. From Portør Panorama you have a great view of the fantastic islands. You can also take a trip up to the pilot's cabin, which is the highest point in Portør. The view from there is impressive. It is easy to see why during the Napoleonic Wars, the coastal defence placed a lookout post and an "optic telegraph" up there. This is now reconstructed and placed in the cabin.

From this place you can continue southwest along the bedrocks. These recreation areas are perfect for picnicking and bathing. Sport fishers will find many tempting places to try their luck at fishing from shore.

Portør is as irresistible and beautiful in autumn as in winter, when the storms whip the houses and the waves wash over the polished rocks.

Portør is one of the best known and much mentioned places in the Levang Peninsula – with good reason as it has much to offer. Just after entering Portør you can take a small side road that will lead you to the beautiful Ospevika churchyard. In this unique environment, you can participate in a moving open-air church service.

Stangnes, between Portør and the crossing at Levang, is also worth a visit. The place is an award winning recreation area with bedrocks and splendid bathing places. You cannot drive the car all the way out, but it is just a short walk. In Stangnes, the Kragerø and Oppland Tourist Organisation has access to an old fisherman's house from the 1870s, where members of the organisation serve coffee and waffles every weekend throughout the summer.

Stangnes

Heading for Risør

The Archipelago of Risør has much to offer, and is a true summer paradise for the sun starved bathers of the north. There is a boat service from Risør Centre to the islands every day during the school holidays.

Risør Sailing Club has a fine marina on Finnøya and you are welcome to use it. There are natural harbours with mooring bolts on the northern and north-western side of the island. Finnøya has sandy beaches and grass plains.

On the inner side of Finnøya is the island Barmen, where you find good harbours. The finest is perhaps Skauholmen, south-west of the island. It belongs to the Coastal Archipelago Park and has a dock and a beach, and you can moor there in all sorts of weather.

Few places along the Southern Coast have a trickier waterway than the one going southwest from Portør. Odd Børretzen's advice about this route is perhaps the best: "You just have to keep well away from the shore until you see the lighthouse and the beacon by Stangholmen." And then you are in Risør. The easiest is often the best, keep to the ship route!

Nevertheless, we have to mention that there is a great inner route that very few people have tried without a local guide. It is mostly suitable for kayaks or small boats with someone constantly on the lookout at the bow. The boat should have a shallow hull, and not be wide. If these conditions are fulfilled, the inner route can be a great adventure.

Levang bay is well worth a visit on a fine day. Storholmen is a fantastic and popular recreation area and has fine sheltered harbours with mooring bolts and good bathing spots.

If you choose to keep your course away from the shore and head for Grønholmgapet, between Grønholmen Lighthouse and Stangholmen beacon, the route ahead towards Risør is open and clean. It is moreover very well signposted for night sailing.

All the way in Gjernes bay – Southwest of Gjernestangen and Pershausen light buoy – you find Myra, which has a fine harbour but somewhat tricky access.

Perleporten (Pearly Gates), which the locals call the narrow strait between Store Vardøya and Lille Vardøya, is a better alternative if you don't mind mooring side by side with other boaters. The entrance to Perleporten from the north is narrow, five metres wide and less than one and a half metres deep. But once you get through, there is a beautiful harbour with great mooring spots. If the boat hull submerges deeper than 1, 3 metres, you have to enter through the south. Because of weak currents, the water is often a few degrees warmer in Perleporten than other places in the outer archipelago. It is a great place for children, with beaches and bathing spots for the little ones. You can also dive for oysters there.

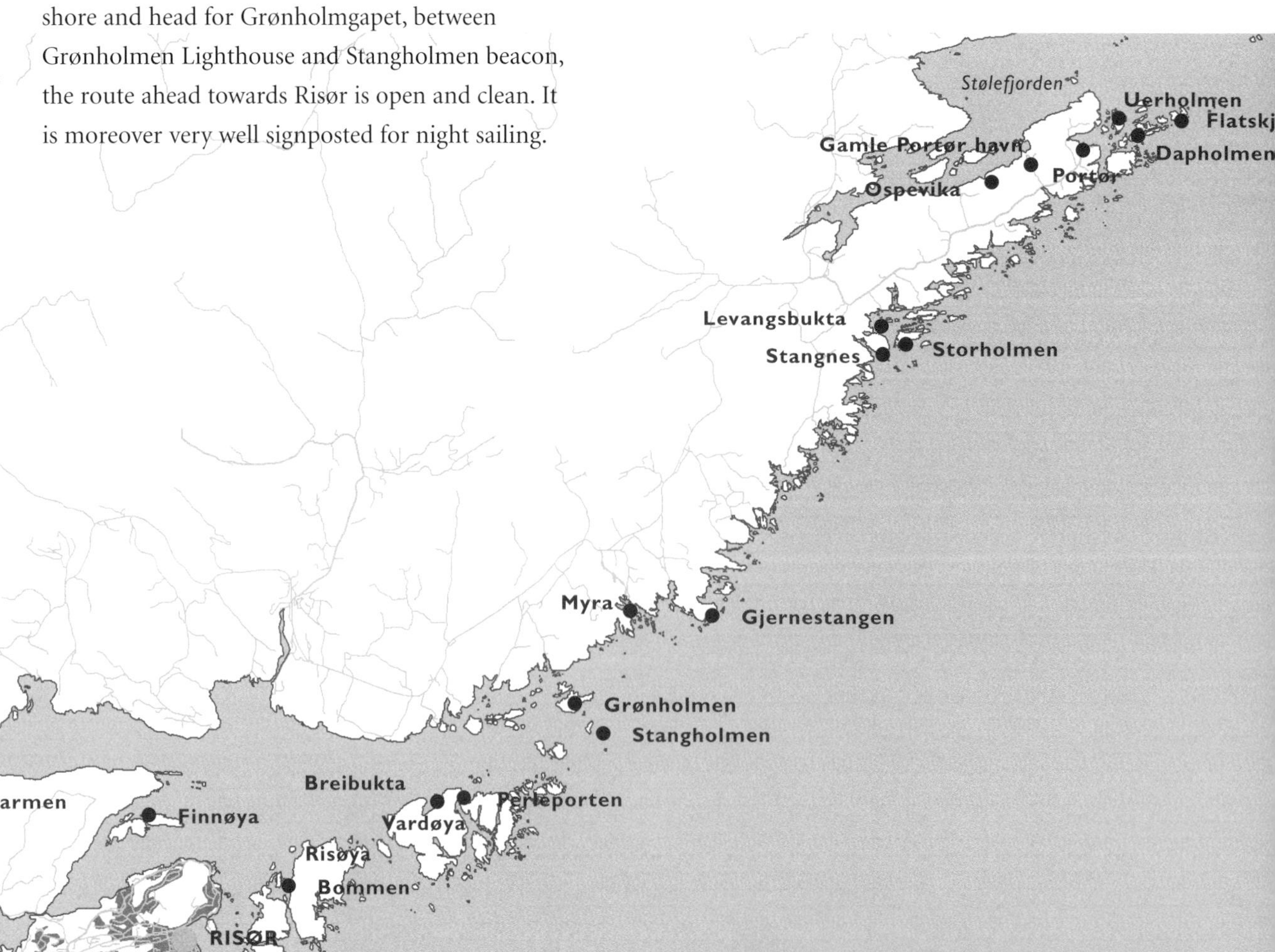

Perleporten

Vardøy bay, the narrow strait between Store Vardøya and Lille Vardøya, is called Perleporten (Pearly Gates) by the locals. Almost the whole area is a public recreation area. Breivika on the northern side of Store Vardøya has docks for visiting boats. Breibukta, north of Vardøya, has many shallow and safe bathing spots for small children.

Pjolterbukta

Risøya, just outside Risør, is owned by Risør Municipality and has large recreation areas. The Risør Motor Boat Club has an impressive dock site, so close to town that you can row there in a light little boat.

The lagoon between Risøy and Langholmen is called Bommen, but it is commonly known as Pjolterbukta ("Longdrink Bay.") Boaters can moor there safely and comfortably and have a short distance to all the facilities: walking paths, playgrounds, volleyball courts, football fields, sandy beaches and indoor dance by fireside.

Many of the islands around Pjolterbukta are fine natural harbours.

RISØR

Risør is among the most beautiful towns in Sørlandet. It is adequately called "the white town by Skagerrak." The distances are short from the town centre to the sea. Among the boaters, Risør is famous for its well organised guest harbour, where all the shops are almost on the pier.

These islands outside Risør create a natural breakwater against the sea, making the town sheltered and safe.

Like many of the other coastal towns, Risør's history started in the sixteenth century with the export of timbre by the Dutch. The massive fire in 1861 burnt the wooden buildings all the way from Solsiden to Tangen to cinders. In all, 248 buildings were burnt to ashes. Since it was prosperous times in Risør, the houses were quickly rebuilt, in similar and "harmonious" architecture. The town also acquired its main streets along the sea, which the visitors highly appreciate.

People in Risør love the skerries. And Risør was among the first places to ensure that the skerries became protected areas. In Lyngholmen we can read the following: "In the year 1933, these islets were awarded to the town of Risør by the East Risøer Workers' Organisation's Support Fund." The conditions were unambiguous: Development must never be allowed!

Today large parts of the Risør skerries are public recreation areas. Talk about being far-sighted! Most of the skerries are freely accessible, providing great prospects for active holidays.

Stangholmen
The lighthouse keeper's dwelling is turned into a restaurant, and the barn is a café.

Festivals
The wooden boat fair and the annual Chamber Music Festival have made Risør known both nationally and internationally. The Chamber Music Festival is very popular and attracts culture journalists from abroad, for example, *The New Yorker* and *The Times*.
For Risør, art and culture have become important areas of focus.

Beside the above mentioned festivals, many are also acquainted with the Villvin handicraft market that takes place each summer in July.

Blackberry is the municipality flower of Risør

Fair-weather islets

Right outside Risøya – north east of Lyngør Lighthouse – you find Risholmene and Terneskjær, also called Flatskjærene. On fine days, this is a "Paradise" on earth for small boats, with plenty of mooring places and sunbathing and swimming spots for big and small. You can jump from the rocks, snorkel, or wade in shallow water, often in "endless" search of crabs. Flatskjærene has it all.

Fielandet and Sild are at the mouth of the fjord, and as in Lyngør, you can find many giant potholes there.

From Risør to Lyngør

The distance from Risør town and out to the open sea is short via Stangholmsgapet. When you have passed Stangholmen Lighthouse you have to cross the open sea for about four nautical miles, because the waters within are shallow and dirty. Therefore, the weather has to be good if you are travelling the distance between Sildodden and Lyngør in a small boat. The area around "Sild" – as it is called locally – can have strong currents, and many people have mixed experiences from there. It is a good idea to make an early start, because even a fresh sunwise breeze can become quite palpable in the afternoon.

If you have to wait for good weather in order to cross "Sild" safely, we recommend a little visit to Sandnesfjorden. Saltbuholmen outside Laukvika is a pleasant and tranquil natural harbour with grass plains and fine rocks. Straight west from Laukvika is Sørlandet Holiday Centre with marina and shops.

Southwest of Risør you pass Fielandet, which has a number of inviting islets and small outer harbours. Fiesund is one of those lovely outer harbours with smooth rocks and small isles, with many fine mooring places.

Åsmundhavn is more exposed, although sheltered from the southwester. From here, it is not far to the famous, giant potholes on Sildodden.

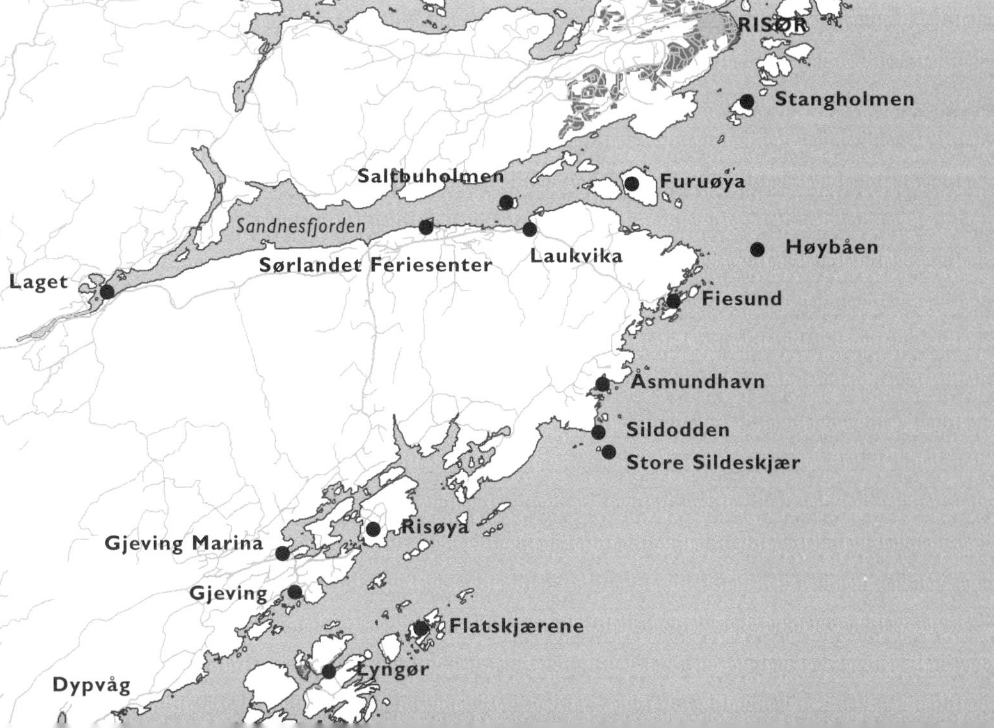

Sailships passing Lyngør lighthouse during Nordic Tall Ships Race.

99

Lyngør

Lyngør is unique. Very few outer harbours have preserved such a characteristic Sørlandet image. The old outer harbour consists of four islands. The largest island, Lyngørsiden, faces Skagerrak. On the inner side, you find Odden and Holmen, and in the west is Steinsøya. The main route between the islands, the long and narrow Lyngør strait – the so-called "street" – is a veritable sight, and not only during midsummer when it is teeming with tourists of all ages. It is also as captivating on a cold, clear autumn day, when the place is shrouded in silent peacefulness.

In Lyngør, the houses are built close to each other along the coast, with their reflections glittering in the sea. Here you find well-manicured gardens, pleasant paths and white picket fences.

All those who come to Lyngør are fascinated by the characteristic buildings, the small idyllic paths and the special wild trees and plants – a heritage left behind from sailors who brought back botanic beauties from their journeys abroad.

In Lyngør, you can only hear the screeching of the seagulls, the fishing boats bumping gently against the pier, or the noise of the youngsters motorboats, and the sound of their clinking bottles.

Lyngør was at its height in the middle of the nineteenth century. In those days, the island was populated with ship owners and skippers living in the elegant whitepainted houses with furniture from the continent.

Grocery shopping

The grocery shop at Lyngør is open from 9 am to 9 pm all week during summer. It is located at the south end of the "street." They have almost everything there, and the shop is the island community's "rumour exchange," with lively discussions taking place both with acquaintances and strangers, which is somewhat unusual in these parts of the country, and therefore extra charming – almost a little exotic.

Seilmakerfruens Kro, the sail maker's wife's café

Lyngør
is accessible only by boat, has no cars, and is known for its scenic harbor and charming wooden houses.
Lyngør is recognized as one of the best-preserved communities in Europe.

You need a boat to get to Lyngør. Local ferries operate regularly, or you can take a taxi boat from Gjeving. For information contact Tvedestrand Tourist Office.

Lyngør is known as one of Europe's best preserved densely populated areas, and the island has about a hundred residents. However, the community is struggling to regulate new housing sites for regular residential areas. People enjoy living in Lyngør, both children and adults, because here they just have to abide to the social democratic "Cardamom Town Law:" Do as you please as long as you are kind and pleasant.

The battle at Lyngør, in 1812, is one of the most dramatic battles in the Napoleonic Wars, surpassed only by the English bombings of Copenhagen. During the whole war, the English warships effectively blockaded any trade between Norway and Denmark. Therefore, in the beginning of 1812, the newly built Danish frigate the *Najaden* was ordered to Norway to strengthen the Southern Coast's defence. The frigate headed southwest from Fredriksvern together with three other sailing ships, and they anchored at Sandøya. However, they were discovered, and the English liner vessel the *Dictator* and three naval vessels sailed towards the entrance to Oksefjorden. The Danish-Norwegian ships sailed to Lyngør, where the Captain of the Najaden chose to anchor. The Dictator followed them and opened fire with its thirty seven canons. The *Najaden* took fire and sunk after two hours of gunfire.

In 1960, the wreck of the *Najaden* was found.

Canon dinghy from the time of the *Najaden*

The Sea Route to Tvedestrand

The sea route to Tvedestrand goes between Borøya and Tverrdalsøya and in Oksefjorden, where you pass Sandvigen. It was here that the composer Richard Wagner sought a port of refuge during a violent storm on 29 July 1839, and was inspired to write the opera *The Flying Dutchman.*

Furøya is an oasis in the fjord and a natural stop on the long trip from Sandvigen to Tvedestrand. This big, charming island with its beautiful buildings and remarkable history is located halfway in Tvedestrandfjorden.

The name comes from the word "fur" which means crack or scar. That is because the island has a number of characteristic cracks all over its surface.

Today, the island is a public recreation area, the closest to Tvedestrand, and popular with both day tourists and those who stay overnight. Furøya is a very friendly island, fun to explore for everyone.

In 1997, Furøya won the prize as the country's best organised recreation area.

It was ship owner Smith from Tvedestrand who built Furøya as a private holiday home for his family. The family owned the island from 1758 to 1945.

The property consisted of Furøya, Hestholmen and Big and Little Furuholmen. It was extremely valuable, because the areas were ideal for storing and preparing timbre.

Today, the island is owned by Tvedestrand municipality and Directorate for Cultural Heritage. In Hestholmen there is an arboretum with many different coniferous trees, brought back by shipowners.

The sailing ship milieu that grew around Oksefjorden-Borøya during the eighteenth century was exceptional. According to the ship lists of Risør Customs from 1780, no less than thirty-four ships used it as their main harbour. The smallest ships sailed to Denmark, while the larger ships transported goods to England. At that time shipping was seasonal. During winter the ships laid up because of snow and ice, but as soon as the ice melted the activity was resumed, freighting timbre, boards and planks.

The maritime milieu in Oksefjorden quickly saw the importance of theoretical education. The skippers' sons often spent the winter in England to learn language, navigation and accounting. One example that education had a high status in the shipping milieu is that King Christian VII gave his approval to the establishment of a private school in Borøykilen in 1799. The ship owners were simply not satisfied with the education the public school could offer, and they took the initiative to start a private school with teachers from Copenhagen. Therefore, it is no coincidence that the country's first sea insurance company, Oxefiordens Gjensidige Søasuranceforening (Ox Fjord's Mutual Sea Insurance Organisation), was established there in 1806.

The oak tree – the great oak tree in the middle of the island is both a playground and a gathering point.

The big buildings in Furøya witness past prosperity

TVEDESTRAND

In Tvedestrand we moor in the guest harbour, centrally located in the middle of the port. Like most towns in the area, Tvedestrand also came into being in connection with the timbre freight in the sixteenth century. But it was the opening of Nes Ironworks in the eighteenth century that really got things going.

The municipality that stretches all the way to Risør in the east and Arendal in the west has a coastal line more than two hundred kilometres long, and no less than 162 islands, where you will find all the summer guests, if they are not running errands in town.

People in Tvedestrand have always looked beyond the horizon. They say that the inhabitants of Tvedestrand were better known abroad than in other parts of Norway. Typically therefore, the lower part of Tvedestrand centre was more important than the upper part, in olden days. It was after all here the trade and business took place, and where people lived. They clung to the steep slopes like birds on a nesting cliff.

The guest harbour in Tvedestrand has everything a boat tourist could ask for. As a curiosity we can mention that the harbour fee includes four fresh rolls for breakfast – delivered with the local paper *Tvedestrandsposten.*

Many summer guests visit *The Nes Ironworks Museum* and the fine golf course, adjacent to the museum. The river Storelva that runs through this area is a salmon river, but is best known for good sea trout fishing.

"The book town of Skagerrak" was established in 2003, and twith a number of second-hand bookshops in the charming and compact wooden buildings, straight up from the harbour. There, most book lovers can find something good. For others it is enough to enjoy the special atmosphere in an intimate book café. You can take your time, since you have sailed the long fjord all the way to Tvedestrand.

The sailing ship town of Tvedestrand has a proud seafaring history. In the New York harbour in the 1870s, there were so many sailing ships registered in Tvederstand that the Americans thought that Tvedestrand must be one of the world's biggest cities. Tvederstrand has never been a cosmopolitan place, but it deserves respect for having been the biggest shipping town in Norway.

The Coastal Culture Week in Tvedestrand is on that exclusive list of Norwegian festivals which are directly funded by the Arts Council of Norway. During the festival there are exhibitions, concerts and historical walks in Tvedestrand, Lyngør, the islands and inland around the town.
The Coastal Culture Week has chosen the tern as its logo. The municipality's coat of arms also has the tern as symbol. The symbolism is good, because like the far travelling tern, both birds and sailors always return to Tvedestrand. At least this was the case with the seamen in this old shipping town.

The Kenilworth ivy is the municipality flower, a ballast plant from the time of the sailing ships. You see them in many stairways and cracks in the walls downtown, but also in a number of other towns along the Southern Coast.

"Strykejernet" (the iron) is one of the most characteristic houses in Tvedestrand.

On the Way to Arendal

From Lyngør to Arendal there are a number of fine routes for boat tourists. A safe and good route is through the Lyngør fjord on the inner side of Askerøya, via Borøya to Oksefjorden. There are many small places with well preserved beautiful houses from the sailing ship era. Dypvåg is one of those places you ought to visit. Make time to walk up to the 700-800 years old beautiful medieval church.

You can also make the trip via Snaresundet on the inner side of Borøya, although it is probably more spectacular on the outer side of Askerøya and Sandøya. Keep going straight from Lyngør and to starboard along the shore of Askerøya, where you will see rows of little gems of nature, for example Nautholmene with its many pleasant spots for overnight stay. If you continue to Sandøya, you will find inviting harbours, bare rocks, sandy beaches, plants, birds and numerous fishing spots. The exterior route off Sandøya is well signposted, and will lead you to magnificent places, such as Håholmen and Fugløya. If you continue southwest towards Holmsund and the beacon at the entrance of Kilsund, you can choose either side of Flostaøya.

Fugløya

Fugløya has much to offer. On the southern end of the island there is a manor like country house, built in 1913 by Ludvig Aadnesen from Tvedestrands, who became rich in England through shipping, but spent the summers at home in his childhood countryside. Aadnesen created a park and paths on the island, planted roses and plants from foreign parts. One can still find foreign plants and see traces of the park.

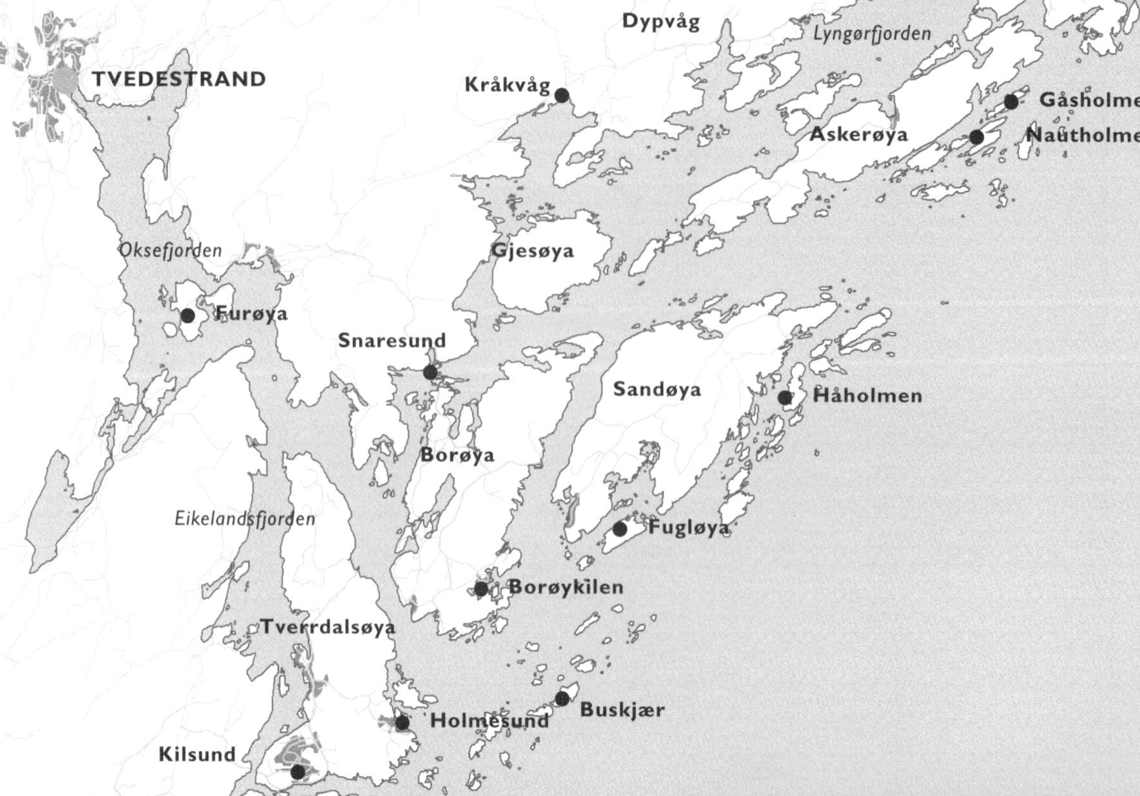

Borøykilen
This is an inviting and agreeable harbour southwest of Borøya.

Buskjæra
When people in Tvedestrand say they are going "out to the rock," they mean Buskjæra, a beautiful brim in the sea, just off the entrance to Tvedestrand.
Buskjæra has characteristic, flat rocks, good mooring places, bathing spots and fresh flora. It also has a teeming bird life.

On fine days, it is superb to stop just before the entrance to Kilsund, where there are some fantastic mooring spots between Buskjæra.

For outings and day trips, Måkeholmene and all the other small islets right off Kilsund are outstanding. On Kalvøya by Kalvøysund you can stay in sheltered lagoons all the way out towards Skagerrak, a summer memory that will last for a long time.

The external route from Kilsund leads westwards to fine harbours in Korshavn, Sandvika and within Skinnfelltangen.

The inner route "Sørlandsleia" via Flosterøya is welcoming and sheltered all the way to Tromøysund.

After Kilsund you follow the route to the lovely Vrangsund, north of Flosta Church. Just before Vrangsund, on the port side, there is a small strait that continues into the sheltered Flostakilen, a large harbour with many mooring spots. The water there is warmer than off Flostaøya and full of oysters.

After Vrangsund, you pass under the bridge to the popular Klokkerøya, a well protected natural beauty and recreation area, with good mooring facilities. Many people spend several nights there, because it is sheltered and the water is usually agreeable.

The route continues towards Arendal through Tromøysund, seven nautical miles long. The locals consider Tromøysund just a passageway, which is rather unfair because there are actually many fine places there, such as the north and east side of Buøya before Eydehavn. Frisøya, at the entrance to Eydehavn, is a great place, especially now that the old smelting plant is shut down.

Right before Tromøybroa by Tromøy, you will find the fine Gjerstadholmene, a good place to stay overnight as an alternative to the Arendal Marina.

Sørlandsleia makes a thrilling S-swing at Vrangsund on the inner side of Flostaøya.

Kalvøya southwest of the entrance to Kilsund has many fantastic fair-weather places.

The sculpture "Sailor's wife with child" greets you as you enter Kilsund.

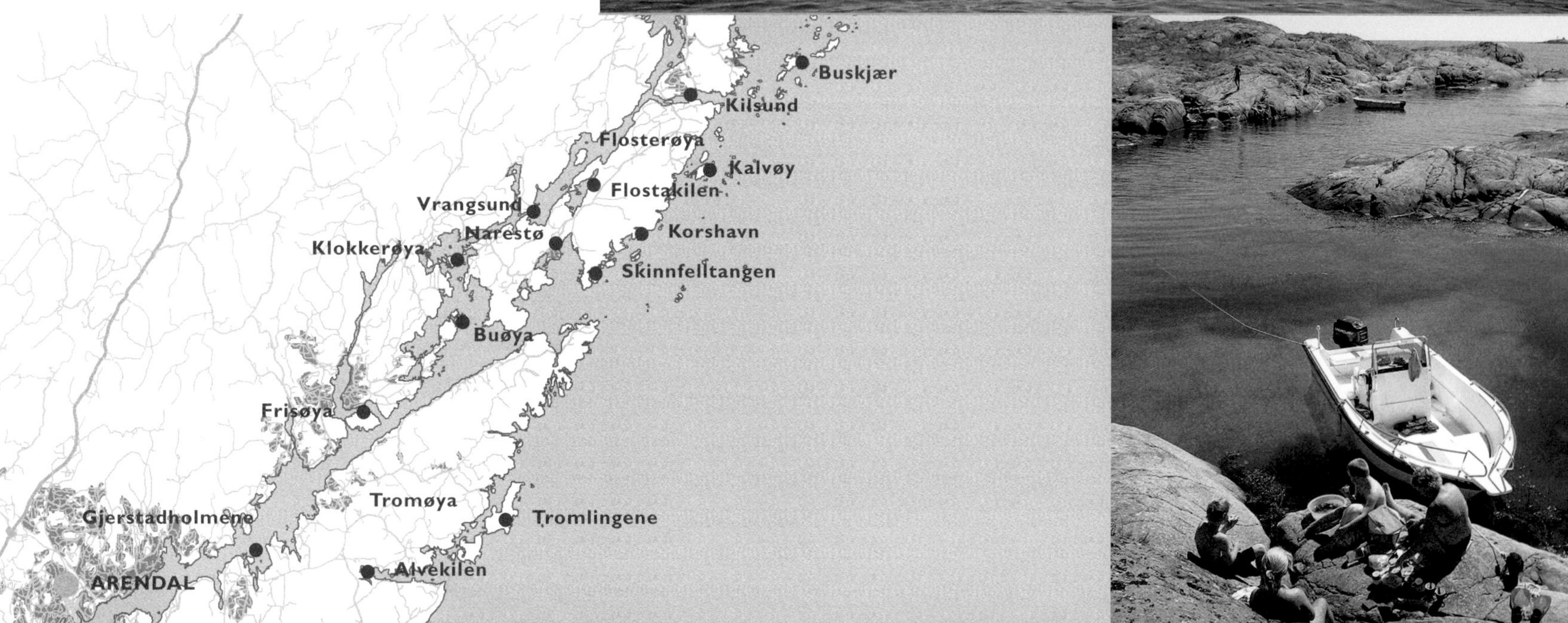

Skinnfelltangen outside the island Flosterøya

Tromlingene

Like Jomfruland, Tromlingene is part of the moraine. Here, you find pebble beaches and taluses, fantastic flora, grazing animals, bird sanctuaries, camping places and above all masses of space.

If you are looking for a special nature experience, you should not sail through Tromøysund. You should head for the open sea outside Tromøya and visit the small island Tromlingene.

Tromlingene is fantastic in all seasons, but at the end of May when the sea thrifts cover the island is the finest.

The best harbour is Tromlingesundet on the west side of Tromlingene, where you will find a small dock and mooring bolts. The island has big grass plains where you can camp or play ball.

There is an easy route further in towards the southwest in Tromlingesundet for smaller boats. It leads to Alvekilen where there are good natural harbours that provide shelter in all sorts of weather.

The route ahead goes across the open sea on the outer side of Tromøylandet. The waters are not difficult to navigate through, but our advice is to keep your distance to the shore. After a couple of nautical miles, you will meet Østregapet to Merdø, and then the route is open in Galtesund to Arendal.

Hove and Hovekilen

All the outer side of Tromøya bears clear traces of the great moraine, the pebble belt that stretches from Vestfold to Fevik. The Tromøy beaches in the southeast are therefore mostly pebbly, bare rocks and cliffs with windswept trees that create a protective forest for the cultivated land beyond.

The protective forest on the outer part of Hove is very special. The ravaging winds have given the pine forest some weird looking formations. Large parts of Hoveodden are protected as part of the moraine landscape protection areas.

There are good bathing spots on the rocks and on the beaches on the inner side of the island. There, you find the quiet and idyllic Hovekilen with its islands, islets and snug bays and beautiful beaches. There are many good places to stay, for instance St. Helena, south of Slåttøya. On the northern end of this islet, you can anchor safely in all weathers.

The waterway is quite clean and suitable both for large and small boats. However, on the northern side of Gjessøya, there is a sand bank that has the irritating tendency to change slightly, once in a while. But if you follow Tromøylandet, you will be all right.

Hove is Aust-Agder's most popular recreation area all year round, not only in summer. In the past years, the Residents' Association in Hove has, in cooperation with Arendal municipality, worked extensively in order to prepare the area for recreation.

Hove has one of the county's most renowned camping sites. The former military camp is almost legendary. The Germans built the camps during WWII. Later, the Norwegian military took over until the early 60s. Thereafter, Hove has been known mostly for its traditional political camps of all kind. There are also cultural camps with main focus on music and song, sports camps, scouts' camps and camps for the disabled – not to mention the numerous motor cycle and veteran car gatherings that are arranged every summer.

The closest neighbour to Hove camp is the beautiful camping place that is snugly situated on the inner side of the Hove headland, where many caravan owners have found their paradise.

All these places are close to Hove's protected areas, with unique natural qualities that are also important historically and geologically. Because the area is Aust-Agder's most visited recreation area, the protected areas are susceptible to wear and tear.

The external side of Hove bears clear traces of the great moraine.

Gjessøya

Gjessøya is a popular island for outings. It is well organised, with a new guest dock, toilets and garbage disposal. You are allowed to camp for two nights in a tent on the fine grass plains with chalk white beaches.

Some families "have the right through common usage" to camp all summer – as they have done for more that thirty-five years!

On the inner side of Hoveodden there are many inviting sandy beaches.

Merdø

The museum pier with Merdøgaard Museum is worth a visit.

If you ask people from Arendal what the most attractive place in the Arendal skerries is, they will reply Merdø without hesitation. You will never regret a trip there, because the Arendal folks are right. This is without doubt one of the gems of the Southern Coast.

The wooden houses in Merdø are well-kept and beautiful, surrounded by orchards and old cultivated land, with laboriously built stone fences.

There are three public docks on the island, but they have relatively few places for visitors. In midsummer it is very crowded. If you visit the island during other seasons or a little early in the day it is easier to find boat places. Moreover, the ferries have several departures from Arendal to Merdø during summer.

There is a very nice café in Merdø, with a sheltered sandy beach by the so-called museum dock. In Merdø you have "to make the rounds," as it is called. It means to walk leisurely through the old neighbourhood's charming paths and streets. You get close to the private properties, but it doesn't matter because here there are both spy mirrors and lace curtains.

The island has also much to offer if you are interested in history. Merdøgaard Museum is an archipelago museum run by Aust-Agder Centre of Cultural History. It is open during summer, when you can visit a unique ship captain's residence from 1736. The interior of the house is well preserved, with original furnishing. The house shows the lifestyle, and particularly the wealth that existed in these outer harbour communities in Sørlandet, such as Merdø. It was not unusual to see the harbour packed with sailboats, where nowadays the odd sailboat is moored to a buoy.

You can find more camping sites on the west side, with grass plains and fine sandy beaches. It is probably easier to find a boat place there. The dock is exposed to wind from the east, the north and the west. If it is gusty, the best thing to do is moor to a buoy, or anchor in the bay outside the museum. There are several buoys available to use for free. Another alternative is to moor at Langerumpa, one of the small the islets at the inside of Merdø.

The pilot's cabin and a canon stand on the island's highest point. A compass rose is carved in the cliff, dated 1654. The pilots probably used it to take the bearing of the direction of the ships that came in. They would then run as fast as they could to jump into the boat, and row or sail at a furious speed in order to help the captain. They worked according to the principle "first come first served."

ARENDAL

At Tyholmen, you will find the old town hall of Arendal, originally the private residence of the rich merchant, Kallevig. The house, which was built in 1815, is the second largest wooden building in Norway. Outside Arendal Old Town Hall is the guest harbour, almost in the centre of the pulsating little town, with its unmistakable city ambience.

Like other towns in the south, Arendal also has a colourful history. During the sail ship period, the town was one of the most important trading towns along the coast, and for a period in the 1870s Arendal was Norway's richest town. In a ballad from that time, the town is referred to as "Kjæmpestaden" (the colossal city,) a name that is today used for the historical festival that is organized at the end of June. The festival shows historical tableaux and markets to depict the lifestyle in eighteenth century Arendal.

During the eighteenth and nineteenth century, the people of Arendal prospered on shipping and timber sales. It is not so strange that Arendal became a junction for these trades, because the town is strategically placed at the mouth of the river Nidelva, and sailing routes both from Galtesund in the south and from Tromøysund in the East.

The old wooden buildings at Tyholmen are absolutely worth a trip, and Arendal town museum "Kløcker's House" gives a proper insight in the way in which wealthy Arendal families lived in the nineteenth century.

Pollen and Tyholmen are meeting places all year round. In the holidays the town is bubbling – literally. Try the freshly poached crabs from the fish boat Snøgg, or sit at a table in one of the many outdoor cafés surrounding Pollen.

Already in May, it becomes the boat people's arena, when the area's yacht producers exhibit their most recent boats at the Sørlandet Boat Fair. The exhibition is organized by Trauma Sports Club, with boats on land, and of course at sea.

At the end of July, the Blues and Jazz Festival comes to town. Canal Street's trademark is to organise the concerts in unconventional and rather spectacular places, such as closed down iron mines, a former train station, and of course at Little Torungen, one of the "the twin lighthouses" you see when sailing in to Arendal.

The poet, Gabriel Scott, settled down in Tromøya in the house called "Maagereiret" (the sea gull's nest), which is situated right by the sea in Galtesund.
Nearby, you find Sørensen's Shipping Museum that can be visited by appointment. Contact the tourist office in Arendal Culture and Town Hall.

Pollen, east of Tyholmen, is one of the trademarks of the town, and the last remains of the canals, which were the town's traffic artery at the time when Tyholmen was a true "holme" – an islet.

Sørlandets Boat Fair takes place in Arendal, at the end of May. All the region's boat builders gather to show the boat enthusiasts the latest in design and equipment.

Norwegian Grand Prix World Championship in Offshore Formula One, is an annual competition that attracts thousands of spectators who wish to experience the Formula one of boat sport at close range.

The lighthouse Little Torungen with Big Torungen in the background

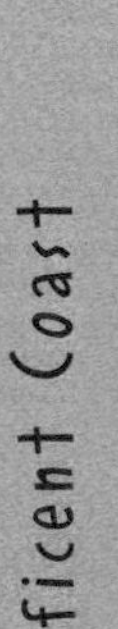

In the Direction of Grimstad

On the way to Galtesund, you go past Søndre Brattholmen, where Arendal Sailing Club is located and has many good mooring places, and their facilities are available for public use. You can spend the night in the lighthouses Torungen and little Torungen on Inner and Outer Torungen. The entrance to the lighthouse harbours is difficult in strong wind and rough sea, but if you have booked your stay through The Norwegian Trekking Association (DNT) in Arendal, they can arrange to bring you back and forth by boat.

From the "Twin Lighthouses" we head towards Grimstad through Havsøysundet. Havsøya is a breathtaking island with classic houses, bare rocks and sandy beaches. There is a magnificent recreation area on the south-western side of the island, called Paradise bay, but it only deserves the name in good weather, because of its exposure to wind from the south and the southwest.

The archipelago and the islets between Arendal and Grimstad have many activities to offer. It is almost impossible to sail past Sømskilen without mentioning Aspholmen, Jerken and Tjuvholmen, perfect places for outings, bathing and camping.

Jerkholmen is like Jomfruland and Tromlingene a part of the visible moraine. There are docks on the northern side of the island, but it is best to moor to buoy within the pebble mounds. There is a fine sandy beach on the southern side. Otherwise, you find cultivated land, grave mounds and a teeming birdlife.

Further to the southwest, you come to Ryvingen and Valøyene with their characteristic red rocks and fine natural harbours. In between these rows of islands is Fevik in the north, all the way inside the narrow bay Fevikkilen, with fantastic beaches, camping sites and one of the most time-honoured hotels in the district.

Hesnesøyene is a natural stopover on the way to Grimstad. In between this delightful outer harbour and the mainland by Hesnes, there are a handful of small and beautiful islets.

Spending the night by the waterway

South of Torungen Lighthouse, at the mouth of the fjord, you find the group of islands called Ryvingen, where you can truly be at one with the sea.
Therefore, we recommend you to stay there in a period with stable weather, because then the conditions are best for bathing, fishing and "crabbing" in the summer nights.
Between the Hesnes Canal, Hesnes and Hesnesøyene there are many fine islets for day trips and for spending the night.

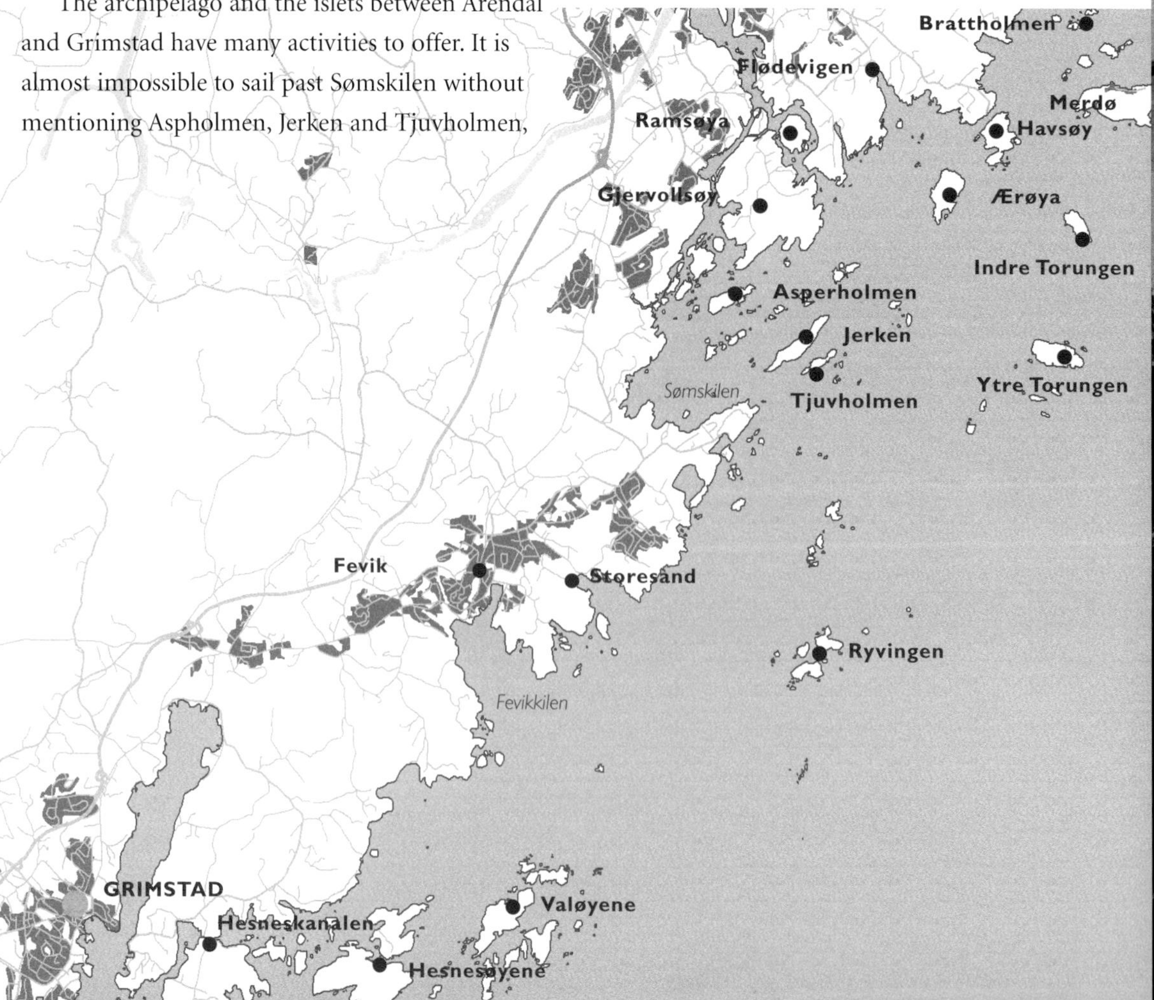

Jerken, or Jerkholmen, separates the inner and outer archipelago west of Arendal. It is almost always calm and quiet in Sømskilen, and you can make the trip through Arendal via Nidelva.

Hesnesøyene

We go on to Hesnessund and the impressive houses in the neighbourhood where the skippers lived. We are in the region of Henrik Ibsen's *Terje Vigen*, the fisherman whom Ibsen supposedly modelled his hero on, in his famous forty three verses.

The place is a popular holiday resort, and both the residents and the cottage owners are proud of their islands' history, whether it is about Christian II who had to seek a safe haven there with his twenty-one ships on his way to re-conquer Norway in 1531, or the history of the dramatic *Charitas* shipwreck, in which Henrik Ibsen's grandfather was killed, in 1760.

Between Hesnesøy and Kvaløya there is a fine harbour with bare rocks, sandy beaches and woods. After Hesnes, you just follow the route, keeping to the starboard in to Smørsundet until you arrive in Grimstad. The route is well marked and easy to follow.

If you have a small boat, you can make the trip to Grimstad via the Hesnes canal. Maybe you will be tempted to stay overnight at Sjursholmen (Fanteholmen) at the mouth of the canal.

Valøyene
Valøyene, straight ahead from Fevik, are big islands with coarse, red Grimstad granite. The Hesnes pyramid, a wooden structure at Kallen, is a well known signpost in the sea in these regions. It is identical with the signpost described in Henrik Ibsen's *Terje Vigen*.
Valøyene have plenty of places for boats, although many big sailing boats have discovered the great natural harbour. The boats are often moored side by side close to the cliffs, or moored at a buoy in the bay.
It was in Valøyene that parts of the film about Gabriel Scott's *Fant* (Vagabond) were shot. Fantebukta is very popular among the local people. The beach is nice and the island is well organised for boat tourists.

Hesnesøyene

GRIMSTAD

It is always a pleasure to come to Grimstad, the town that is fondly called "the pearl of Sørlandet." It seems like many people who come to Grimstad prefer to stay at the pulsating and social guest harbour, rather than in one of the natural and peaceful harbours. In Grimstad you can choose whichever, because the conditions are perfect, both in the guest harbour and the beautiful skerries outside the town. These past years, there have been remarkably fewer boats mooring by the islands within the skerries. The reason may be that Grimstad has one of the country's finest guest harbours with many facilities and activities for families. There is both a bowling alley and go-cart tracks in town. The schooner, Solrik, organises pirate raids on the islands. And the traders tempt the customers with market days.

The midsummer night festivities are unique in these regions. It seems that all the residents and the tourists from miles away gather to celebrate Midsummer Eve in the skerries. The festivities begin early in the evening with the congregation of an armada of small boats in the inner harbour. The boats are decorated with flowers of all sorts, and they parade through the regular route in honour of all the spectators, with the accompaniement of accordion music filling the harbour.

When Ibsen went to work as an apprentice for the chemist in Grimstad, he fell in love with the town. Many characters of his plays are based on figures from this little southern town. Each year, Grimstad town arranges the Ibsen Days, and one summer day people are invited to Hesnes to listen to the dramatic declamation of *Terje Vigen*. The open air theatre outside the town, Fjæreheia, is also quite famous, and it is quite an experience to watch a performance in the old stone quarries – whether it is an Ibsen classic or something completely different.

The Hesnes Canal
With a small boat it is a pleasant and exciting trip through the Hestnes Canal, from Hesnes past Marivold Camping and in to the town fjord via Rønnes.

From Grimstad to Lillesand

It is a very short distance from Grimstad to good stopovers in the archipelago. Keep to the starboard in the middle of the Smørsund bay and head westwards towards Maløyene.

Between Ytre Maløya og Indre Maløya there is a beautiful place to visit, commonly known as "Kalven" (the Calf). In this recreation area you are welcome to stay several days, and it is possible to make small trips to town in the dinghy to shop or eat at one of Grimstad's many pleasant restaurants.

If you are heading southwest, across Groosefjorden, you can explore Bufjorden with its cosy harbours or head off to the sea.

Strandfjorden with the Reddal Canal may be a stimulating alternative if it is very windy. The canal starts inside the fjord and is suitable for motorboats with shallow hulls submerging less than one metre.

If you sail outside the archipelago westwards to Homborsund Lighthouse over "Homborsider," the journey is simple and manageable, because the coastal route is well signposted. However, be aware that this is a part of the sea route for which many people have great respect. In good weather the crossing is very easy, but with wind and rough sea it can become rather unpleasant for small boats.

By Homborsund Lighthouse the most beautiful route is undoubtedly the one going furthest out. Head towards the open sea, past the lighthouse, keep to the starboard and sail carefully through the narrow waterway between Homborø and Kongsholmene. There, you will see some gorgeous sandy beaches, inlets and bays – irresistible places to spend a day or two.

Kalvøyene is located on the east side of Homborøya and on its west you find Ålesøya, which has a fantastic lagoon towards the western end of Homborøya.

Auesøya, big and little Malmen are also very popular places in the Lillesand Archipelago, because the islands have many bedrocks, sandy beaches and good mooring places. Eastern Hestholmbukt, southwest of Skogerøya, is one of the most visited places. So is Lamholmen, just before the entrance to Lillesand.

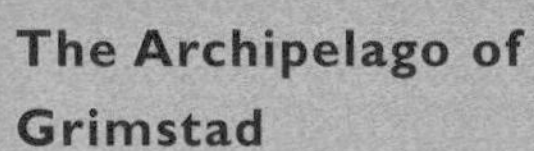

The Archipelago of Grimstad

In this archipelago the gems are lined up, among them Lille Hampholmen to the south of Smørsundet. Also "Kalven," the rounded fjord between Store Maløya og Lille Maløya, is a snug and lovely place. There are docks for those who want grass fields to play football on or to camp. Like in Risør, the recreation areas outside Grimstad were protected for public use quite early. "The Residents' Association of Grimstad Town" played an important role, and the works begun early around 1920. Today, both the local population of Grimstad and all the visitors enjoy the results.

Homborsund Lighthouse

Ytre Maløya

Morning mood from Rivingen Lighthouse by Grimstad

Rivingen Lighthouse

Auesøya

The boat route to Lillesand is simple and clean. However it is also possible to go via Grunnesund, which is not as shallow as one may imagine, because the clear water and the sandy bottom that reflects light can be deceiving. But it is narrow. You can go in by Svertingen through big and little Malmen. If the wind blowing from the south-west is strong, it is often a good idea to avoid sailing round the red stake in Indre Malmgrunnen.

In this part of the skerries, there are many bathing spots and safe harbours before Lillesand. The most popular harbours are Østre Hestholmbukta southeast of Skogerøya or Lamholmen right before you get to Lillesand.

Many people choose to make the trip directly to Auesøya and Skogodden, or "Sokken," (the sock) as the locals call this popular public recreation area. The island is at the outmost end of the skerries towards the open sea, on the borders of Grimstad and Lillesand municipalities.

The island is a gift from high court attorney, Henrik Lundh in Oslo to Grimstad municipality. In 1984, sixty-four decares of the island became a protected area. The recreation area on the south side of the island has fresh and clean water for bathing, and the sandy beach inside the bay is of the finest sand and very shallow water, making it ideal for small children.

On the southwest side of the island there is a bay facing the open sea. Therefore large amounts of rubbish and floatage from the sea gather there. Lillesand municipality has decided not to do anything about that to show people the amount of rubbish the sea currents leave behind along the Southern Coast.

Auesøya is a typical southern island with beautiful nature and cultivated land and rich flora and fauna. There you find snug inlets, sandy beaches and woods. For those interested in plants, Auesøya is probably best known for its many daffodils, and is therefore a popular destination for botanists, clubs, and associations, particularly during the spring bloom. The island is very fertile with 254 different registered plant species. Among heat loving plants we find English ivy, honeysuckle, oak, hazel, sweet cherry and yew.

Auesøya has fine, clearly signposted walking paths through a landscape of grave mounds, plains and farmlands surrounded by stone fences. Lillesand municipality takes care of the cultivated landscape by regularly clearing the land and having sheep graze in the area.

There is a brochure about the place, and information boards that mark the natural trails and the constructed paths.

Auesøya is without doubt the boaters' paradise, but also those who do not have a boat can enjoy this fertile and beautiful island right on the edge of the open sea. Contact the tourist office in Grimstad, alternatively the town gardener's office, and you will definitely get help to get to get to Auesøya and back again.

Skogodden on Auesøya is also called "Sokken" where it is extremely pleasant to lie snugly and safely at the outmost edge of the open sea.

Auesøya is known for its wild daffodils and white narcissus.

LILLESAND

Lillesand reflects the urban society of the sailing ship era, where the ship owners and the traders had central properties by the sea. Behind the fine facades were the outhouses for town farming.

Lillesand has kept many of the old wooden buildings from the eighteenth and nineteenth century. The immaculately kept white houses stand in rows in the town centre. Many of the large manor houses in the centre are today listed buildings. *Henschiengården* still functions as the town hall. Another manor house, *Carl Knudsengården*, is turned into a fine maritime and town museum, which shows Lillesand's development from a summer resort to an important shipping town. Lillesand has no less than three churches from the twelfth century.

The town has a cosy and harmonious ambience, and it is a pleasure to stroll in the streets and the harbour, visit a pastry shop, and rest on a pleasant bench in the little park.

The harbour in Lillesand is pleasing and easy to navigate in, and the new guest harbour has place for two hundred boats, with all the facilities that the boaters require. The new fish shop inside the harbour is commendable and the butcher in the high street has first class stuff. The bakery Knudsen and Rønnevig has delicious custard tarts.

Lillesand has a pleasant town beach located in the middle of the town harbour. Here, the kids can play and have fun while you relax with a cup of coffee and a bun, or freshly cooked shrimps.

Lillesand is the gateway to Blindleia, but we recommend that you take a trip to the Lillesand skerries before setting off towards Blindleia. You will discover small inlets and idyllic places few people do, because they are so concentrated on getting to the famous Blindleia. Maybe you can be lucky and find your own little summer place where you can moor at a buoy and do what the celebrities do in their expensive cottages, take the dinghy to town to go to a pub, the restaurant or an art exhibition. You can then feel a little like a tourist and a little like a local resident.

Dog rose is Lillesand's municipality flower.

Saltholmen lighthouse
The lighthouse marks the entrance to Lillesand through Sandsgapet. The lighthouse was built in 1882, and is owned today by Lillesand Sailing Club.
The name Saltholmen (salt islet) comes from when the philanthropist, Hans Nielsen Hauge, rented it during depression years in 1809-10, to teach coastal people to produce salt from saltwater.

Blindleia

Many people have used grand words to describe Blindleia. Gabriel Scott, who grew up in Høvåg in the middle waterway, calls it "the finest gem of the skerries."

Today, it is trendy to own a property in Blindleia and the prices for recreational properties have become absurd – to put it mildly.

The insurgence of the market forces can easily take the focus away from the characteristic values of the 'real' Blindleia, as described so vividly and with such warmth by Gabriel Scott in his book *Kilden.* For it was precisely in these waters, in and around Blindleia that Markus, the hero of the book, travelled with his unassuming boat. There, he lived ascetically in tune with nature. Each day, he fetched just enough from 'Our Lord's larder' for his dinner, and perhaps just a little more, in order to exchange with his neighbours and acquaintances things he needed.

Blindleia is perhaps the most mentioned area in the Southern Coast. It stretches from Lillesand to Gamle Hellesund and is about six-seven nautical miles long. You can sail through it in an hour or so, but many people prefer to stop over, because there are so many idyllic places to see. The whole waterway is perfectly signposted, and the greatest danger is the congested traffic during the holidays. The weeks before and after are quiet – remarkably quiet – and many of the fantastic properties are locked and bolted.

As soon as you sail under Justøybroa, the waterway becomes narrow. Nevertheless, it is beautiful and is what the southerners call "snugly cosy."

During summer the boat traffic is busy both ways, because of the uninhabited and popular Mortensholmen just after Justøybrua. The boats are on their way to, or are returning from, Brekkestø, Ågerøyhamn and Gamle Hellesund, which are very well-known places in Blindleia.

Brekkestø is one of the truly finest outer harbours in Blindleia. During the sailing ship era, there could be as many as ninety ships moored in the harbour in Brekkestø in winter. You still can see some of the mooring rings from that time many places around the harbour.

Brekkestø was an international harbour with sailing ships from England, Holland, Germany and Russia. There were hundreds of sailors to cater for, and the need for shops, pubs, and inns was bigger than today. Nowadays, Brekkestø is the summer tourists' paradise. There are still boarding houses and shops here, but the pubs are history.

The best harbours near Brekkestø are the ones closest to the open sea. They are all there on the outer part of Ågerøya, one little gem after another: Meholmen, Burholmen with Knutshavnsundet, Vadbuholmen right outside the idyllic Ågerøyhamn. The latter is well worth a visit for those who are interested in the outer harbours of the sailing ship era. In the beautiful harbour, most of the houses are well preserved and unchanged since the eighteenth and nineteenth centuries.

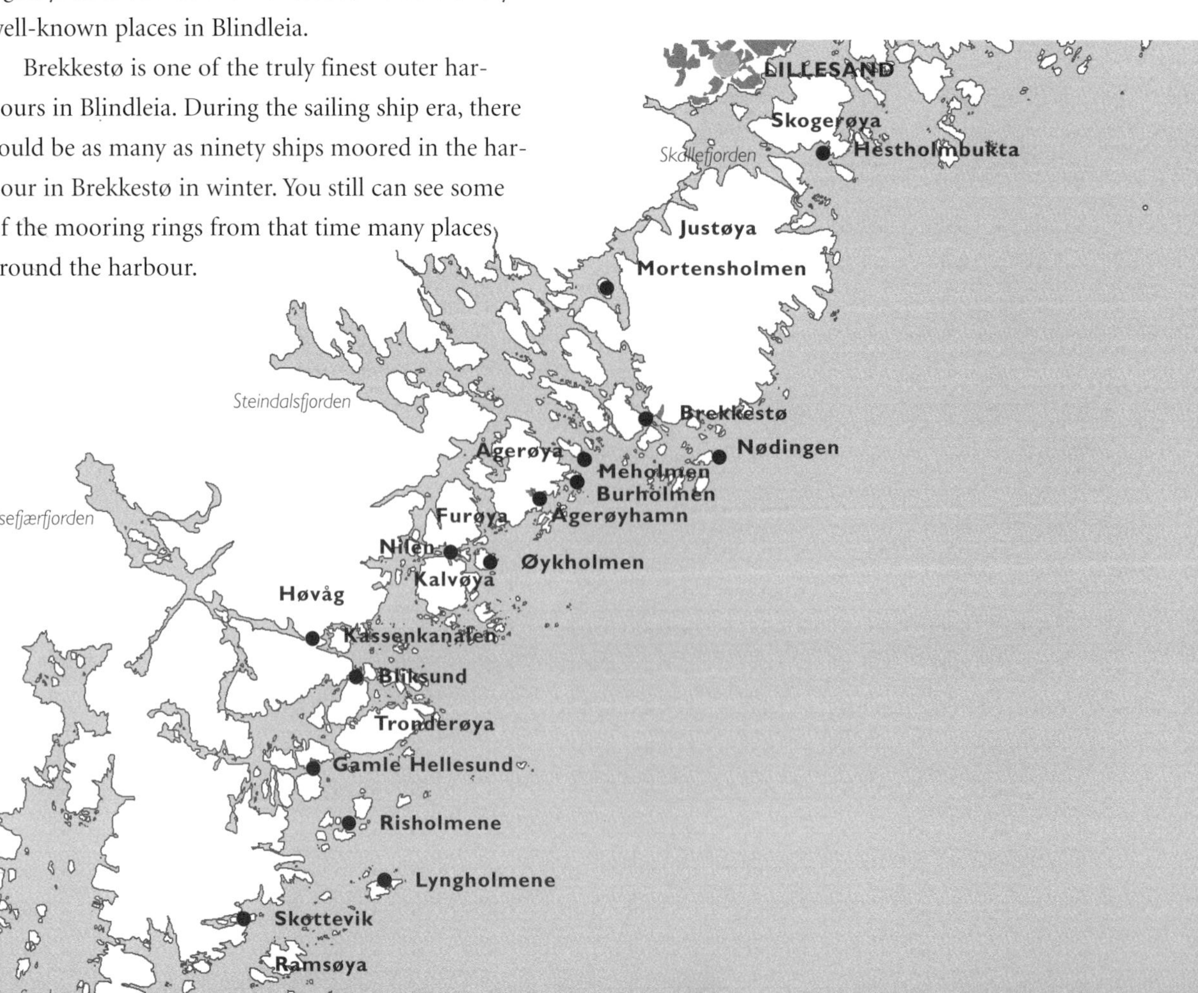

Blindleia is undoubtedly a southern gem and the boaters love this cosy route that swings on the inner side of the wooded islands, and past known places such as Brekkestø, Ågerøyhamn, Gamle Hellesund and Ulvøysund.

Brekkestø

It is said that during the sailing ship era, Brekkestø was the most visited harbour in Sørlandet because of its proximity to the open sea. Therefore, even today you can see the residences of the skippers and the mooring rings everywhere, as a proof of the grand old days. In those days, there were also several inns that served food and home brews to hungry and thirsty souls. In these communities the pilots were important and powerful men. The painter Christian Krohg found many of his pilot motives precisely in Brekkestø.

The powerful mooring rings and bolts on all the cliffs show that Gamle Hellesund was a popular harbour during the sailing ship era. Each ring represents a solid income for the owner, and for many seamen widows this was a proper widows' pension. The ship owners that had to have their ships moored for winter had to pay rent to those who owned the mooring rings.

The harbour is as it has always been, blissfully lacking all the modern facilities such as guest harbours and marinas. For what is the point, when you have all the free mooring rings and bolts available there?

Gamle Hellesund is also famous for having been an important storage place for lobsters. The lobster trade can be documented all the way back to the time when the Dutch were there, and the lobster traps were laid out in rows. Owning a 'lobster farm' was like having money in the bank. At most, there could be up to ten thousand lobsters in these traps.

The island communities come to life when the outer harbours Brekkestø, Ågerøyhamn and Gamle Hellesund are invaded by the holiday makers at midsummer.

Blindleia is fine, but beyond Blindleia there are also many idyllic places. Certainly, the fantastic spots here are more exposed to wind and storms, but on the other hand you can experience the true essence of the joys of boating.

The waterways around Kalvøy south of Furø are beautiful when the weather is good. Between Furøya and Kalvøya there is a narrow and shallow strait, called "The Nile," and if you have a boat that does not stick down deeper than half a metre, you can sneak back to Blindleia through this inlet.

At the entrance of "the Nile," you will find the well organised Øykholmen, where there are many fine mooring places.

Around Tronderøya and by Risholmene and Lyngholmene south of Gamle Hellesund there are many fine natural harbours, which are worth exploring in good weather.

Brekkestø

Gamle Hellesund

The characteristic signpost at Nødingen is Brekkestø's trademark facing the open sea. It was set up in 1825, after a shipwreck. The wooden signpost burnt down in the1960s, but was later rebuilt and is now maintained by Brekkestø's Resident Association.

On the outside of Ågerøya there are many "good weather" spots such as here at Knutshavn.

Ågerøyhamn
Ågerøyhamn outer harbour is a jewel on the outer side of the island. We can warmly recommend a stroll through the many paths. You can moor by the public dock on the southern side of the island and begin your walk from there, but be aware that the ferry has its own reserved place.

Ramsøya

Heading for Kristiansand

After Gamle Hellesund we quickly approach Ulvøysund, another magnificent outdoor harbour, which has been transformed into a beautiful recreation area with great bedrocks. It is particularly nice at Kroksundlandet, where you have a fantastic view eastwards through Ulvøysund.

There is often a rough crossing when you get to Kvåsefjorden. Therefore, it is a good idea to start off early in the morning when crossing the open sea over Kvåsefjorden. An ordinary sunwise wind in the afternoon can become unpleasant for those who travel in small boats in these waterways.

On the way to Kristiansand there are many good harbours by Maløya in Kvåsefjorden and to the southwest of Torsøya at the tip of Randøysundet. There is an unbelievably beautiful lagoon.

Nevertheless, Stokken and the islands outside Randøyene are the most popular on that route. All the area by Kalvøyene south-west of Randøya is part of the Coastal Archipelago Park. There are good mooring places and great bathing spots. It can be exhilarating to navigate through "The Needle's Eye" north of Haraldviken and west of Randøya. Skippergada, the delightful bay between eastern and western Randøy, is also worth a visit.

Grønningen Lighthouse is on the east side of Østergapet at the entrance of Kristiansand. The lighthouse should only be visited on fine days because it is difficult to get to the harbour when the sea is rough. You can book a place to spend the night at the lighthouse via Bragdøya Coast Club.

Dvergsøya has a sheltered and good harbour with a dock and mooring bolts in the cliff. The island is part of the Coastal Route, Kystleden, and you can spend the night in "Miljøboden," or camp on the grass fields on the island. There are ferries to and from Dvergsøya from Kristiansand during summer. North-west of Dvergsøya you see a number of magnificent small islands and islets in the Coastal Archipelago Park. Prestøya is part of the Coastal Route, Kystleden, and the Motorboat Club and Sailing Club in Kristiansand have built a dock for free use. It is a great place to camp with fantastic bathing spots.

Grønningen Lighthouse

Grønningen Lighthouse at the outmost end of Kristiansand Fjord is open to the public. The lighthouse is on a little island called Øya. Part of the island is a protected bird sanctuary from 15 April to 15 July. Since public transport boats are not allowed to enter the windswept lighthouse harbour, it feels rather "exclusive" to come to Grønningen. But people come in kayaks, rowing boats, sailing boats and motorboats. Bragdøya Coastal Club has forty sleeping places and you can borrow a rowing boat.

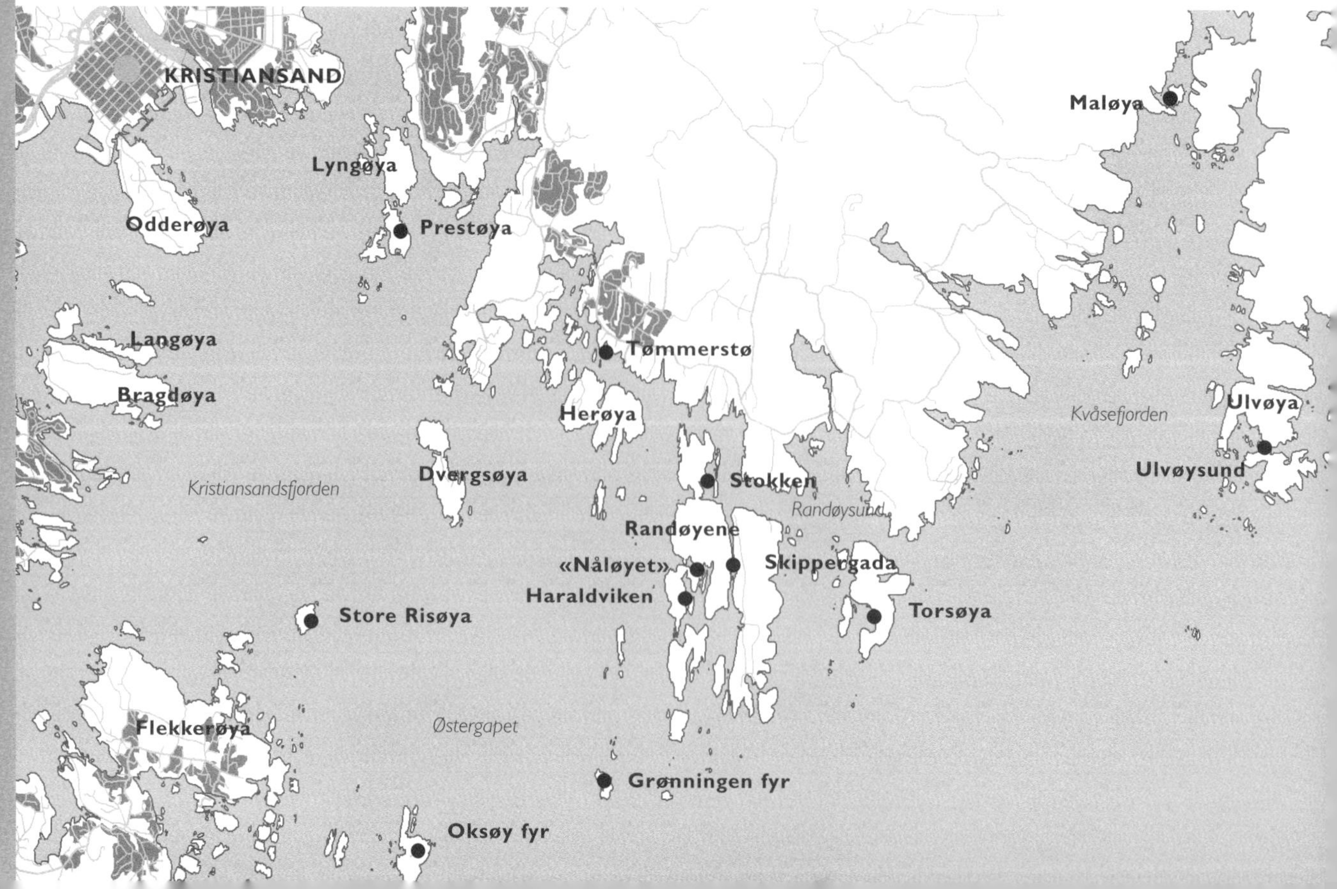

Ulvøysund
marks the beginning of the Archipelago of Kristiansand.

Stokken
is just separated from Østre Randøy by a narrow strait. It is the property of the Kristiansand Municipality and is used as a public recreation area, well organised for boaters.

Skibbergada (left) between Østre Radøy and Vestre Randøy is one of the architectural attractions of Kristiansand. Manor houses are lined up on each side.

Grønningen lighthouse

KRISTIANSAND

Kristiansand is the capital of Sørlandet, the biggest town in the southern coast and the home harbour for *S/S Sørlandet.* You can see all this as a boat tourist, because the harbour to the east of Odderøya is spacious, with plenty of space for both big and small boats. There are showering and laundry facilities, a park by the sea with artworks by the local artist, Kjell Nupen. It is a well-organised harbour, but the "cosiness" you find in many of the other southern towns is not quite the same in the guest harbour of Kristiansand. On the other hand, you can find idyllic places if you stroll uptown and visit the old part in the Kvadraturen.

Christian IV certainly demanded order when he had the town built in 1641. He had the town centre divided into fifty-four blocks with seven streets running parallel to the sea, and ten streets crossing these at right angles.

After the town fire, the old wooden houses were rebuilt in bricks, and the buildings that survived the ravages of the fire have been finely restored.

Christian IV also built Christiansholm fort in the 1660s. The fort, from which reportedly only one shot has been fired, is the closest neighbour to the guest harbour run by the Sailing Club.

Parts of the Odderøya are recreational areas, and

both in Bendiksbukta and in Kjerregårdsbukta there are fine bathing spots. This is where the Quart Festival, which is the highpoint of the summer for the younger generation, takes place. If you have teenagers on board, it is not easy to keep them nearby when the youth culture takes over the town, casting an echo all over the archipelago.

It is a must to visit Markensgate when in Kristiansand. This pulsating high street that stretches all the length of the town centre is an adventure in summer. It is only a five minutes walk from the harbour to Markens.

Families with children are of course attracted by Dyreparken, the Zoo, Norway's most visited amusement park.

The guest harbour is situated on the east side of Odderøya. There is plenty of space and the service centre has all the facilities. The harbour is surrounded by a beautiful park and it is a short distance to the restaurants, the town beach and Markens, Kristiansand's lively shopping street.

Nupen-parken or Otterdalsparken is a beautiful park by the guest harbour. The Kristiansand artist Kjell Nupen's monumental portals in granite are surrounded by fountains.

Fiskebrygga – the fishing wharf is a lively meeting place with outdoor restaurants and busy boat traffic.

Southwest of Bragdøya

On the way to Kristiansand, you ought to visit Bragdøya. Bragdøya and Langøy have huge recreation areas and are very popular in all seasons except winter. There are regular ferries to the islands.

Bragdøya is permeated with coastal culture. It is wholly owned by Kristiansand Municipality and is the starting point for the Coastal Route, Kystleden, in Kristiansand and Søgne. There are restaurants and meeting rooms in the large boathouses. Earlier, these boathouses were used for salting and storing mackerel. Therefore, a great exhibition about the history of mackerel fishing in Sørlandet has acquired its natural place there.

Kongshavn in the south is the best harbour in Bragdøya. It has safe mooring spots and fine camping places on the island, with beaches and bedrocks. This is a small paradise right outside the capital of Sørlandet. Indeed, not only a summer paradise, because the children in Bragdøya Nature Kindergarten romp around there all year round, together with other schoolchildren from town. Like master landscape gardeners, hardy wild sheep graze outside all year round and help keep the cultural landscape in pristine shape.

Kystleden – The Coastal Route

Kristiansand has organised environmentally friendly outdoor activities along the coast, by providing stopovers for overnight stay, and the possibility to rent traditional rowing boats. You can row from place to place and spend the night in Bragdøya, Dvergsøya, Stokken and Grønningen Lighthouse.

Of course, you can use your own sea jeep if you are not wild about the nostalgic boat life with squeaky oars and the smell of tar. Contact Mid Agder Recreation Council or Bragdøya Coastal Club (Kystlaget) for more information.

Bragdøya Coastal Club is located in the boathouses north west of Bragdøya. They also administer Grønningen Lighthouse.

In addition to the many great rowboats, Bragdøya Coastal Club has also the responsibility for three covered vessels that all have the status of being worthy of preservation. These are: the sailing ship "*Dagma*," which is an old pilot smack from Flekkerøya. The motor smack "*Pil*" is built in Barmen in Risør, and so is "*Nesebuen*," which is used by fishermen from Flekkerøya. All vessels are of caravel type fishing smacks from the first half of the twentieth century.

All of Bragdøya with its neighbouring islets are public recreation areas, altogether more than 225 acres.

Flekkerøya

Flekkerøya is rather exceptional with its miniature archipelago surrounding the island.

It is the biggest island in the Kristiansand Archipelago and is connected with the mainland through a 2327 metres long tunnel. Flekkerøya has a number of bathing places and places to moor. Try the south western side of Outer Flekkerøy, where you will find a number of bays and inlets. However, the waterway can be tricky. Tjamsøya and Romsvika on the mainland are fantastically fine places (see map on page 242).

In the strait between Flekkerøya and Flekkerøyhamn you find the little fortress island Fredriksholm. There are good camping sites within the walls and the trenches are covered with vegetation. If you set off towards the mainland and Møvig, you will come to one of the finest recreation areas in the region, coves with fantastic bathing spots, undisturbed and hidden from the view of the surrounding islets.

The small peninsula at Bestemorsmed protects an idyllic little beach, which is a fine place to be when the weather is at its best.

There is a proposition to make a canal through Flekkerøya between Lindebøkilen and Mæbøfjorden. A canal will undoubtedly better the boaters' access to the Outer Flekkerøy with its surrounding skerries.

In the large photograph to the right you see Grønningen and Oksøy lighthouse on the horizon. Oksøy lighthouse is also worth a visit. We recommend you make an appointment with the lighthouse keepers for a visit. Except for the area around the lighthouse, it is forbidden to go ashore in Oksøy and the little surrounding islands until 15 July.

Hellevika, a little paradise on earth on the inner side of Flekkerøya

The Archipelago of Søgne

The archipelago of the coastal municipality Søgne consists of 1229 islands, islets and bedrocks. It is probably the widest archipelago along the whole Southern Coast. Here there are a number of big and small islands, many of them perfect for bathing and boating.

The most known place in these waterways is Ny-Hellesund and the famous strait called Olavssundet. This is one of the largest and best organised recreational areas in the Archipelago of Søgne. You can get there by ferry from Høllen if you do not have a boat yourself.

Many seems to believe that New Hellesund marks the end of the Southern Coast, as we like to think of it with rounded rocks and cosy bays. We will not discuss this any further except say that the nature changes remarkably in character. But you will find fantastic places that clearly have the characteristics of Sørlandet. This coastline has the widest archipelago of the South Coast of Norway. We are approaching Mandal.

In Ny-Hellesund you can find a rare stone figure in the ebb-tide. Is it a man, a fish, a whale, or a monster? The Danish sculptor, Claus Ørntoft, has placed the eight ton granite sculpture *Introspective Stranding* between the stones in the shallow end of the Dødmannsbukta on Kapelløya in Ny-Hellesund, and the county governor in Vest-Agder has given his "blessings."

The sculpture is there to stay in the archipelago. Whether it is there to mark the transition from the soft coastal line to the more rugged Western Coast is hard to tell, but the artist can surely give an answer. No matter what, it is rather amusing and surprising.

Introspective Stranding,
Sculpture by Claus Ørntoft from Denmark.

The ferry trips
Ferries and sightseeing boats to and from Høllen, the junction in the Søgne archipelago, to Ny-Hellesund, Olavsundet and Borøy

Ny-Hellesund

Ny-Hellesund is known for its harbour pilotage, particularly due to the artist Amandus Nielsen's painting *Morning in Ny-Hellesund*, but also because of the fine houses of the captains, which stand as monuments from the grand era which the southerners are proud of, with good reason.

Generally, it is difficult to find a dock in Ny-Hellesund, but small boats can safely enter through the north, between Kapell and Helleøya.

Notice the monograms and profiles on the cliff sides of Helgøya. The legend says that when King Olaf the Holy sought refuge in Ny-Hellesund, the mountain opened and let the King pass through to safety from the enemies that were at his heels. In Olavsundet, you can see the profile of King Olaf the Holy on the cliff sides, where also the King's monogram has been carved.

Just as you leave the bay, you will notice an idyllic lagoon with fine sandy beaches, grass fields ideal for camping and ball games, and a number of safe places to stay overnight. If you can choose, stay at Kapelløya where you are protected from the sunwise wind, which can be blustery in the afternoon.

The royal monograms carved in the mountainside under the "profile" of King Olaf the Holy.

Ny-Hellesund has been a particularly important harbour since the Viking era. Two large monumental beacons were raised on Helløy in the eleventh century. One believes that it was Olaf the Holy who ordered them. During WWII, the German occupational forces destroyed the beacons, which are now rebuilt in concrete.

Towards Mandal

If you continue the trip to Mandal by heading to the Lindesnes Lighthouse and to Farsund, you won't regret it, because in the continuation of the wonderful Archipelago of Søgne you arrive at Mandal. You notice that the sea is more turbulent, the water temperature a couple of degrees lower and the wind somewhat cooler. At the same time, the archipelago acquires a wonderful freshness.

From New Hellesund and further westwards, there are a number of fine natural harbours in succession.

Udvår, or Uvår as the locals call it, is a must to see, because although the group of islands is windy at the mouth of the fjord, there are a number of fine and sheltered harbours, for example Udvårkilen. Vassøyene in the south of Ålo has also many good spots.

Mandal Municipality administers several more sheltered stopovers, among them Fugløya. It is not easy to recommend harbours in this fine area. Nevertheless, we can mention the islands just off Tregde Marina and Holiday Centre. Sandøya is well organised, and so is Sæsøyholmene east of Sandøya. South of Sandøya is Odd, the most southerly point in the Norwegian waterways.

You may also explore the surrounding areas of Ryvingen Lighthouse. The Mandal Archipelago is just fantastic, and the good thing about it is that there is plenty of space for all those who are looking for a place to enjoy a few leisurely days.

Far out to the south

When the weather is stably fair and warm, you may want to take the trip out to sea and visit Odd, the island south of Sandøya. If you moor in Langvika at Odd, there will be no place further south, because it is the southernmost natural harbour and recreation area. The area is well prepared, and the rocks are inviting. There is a good bathing place for children in the innermost end of the bay. But if you wish to stay overnight, we recommend Sandøybukta on the west side of Sandøy – towards Skjøringa – where you will be able to moor relatively sheltered.

South-west of Odd is Oddknubben, or Pysa, which many people consider as the southernmost point of Norway.

Farestad

Udvår
This island is located at the outmost end of the archipelago between Ny Hellesund and Mandal, and has idyllic natural harbours – certainly worth a visit.

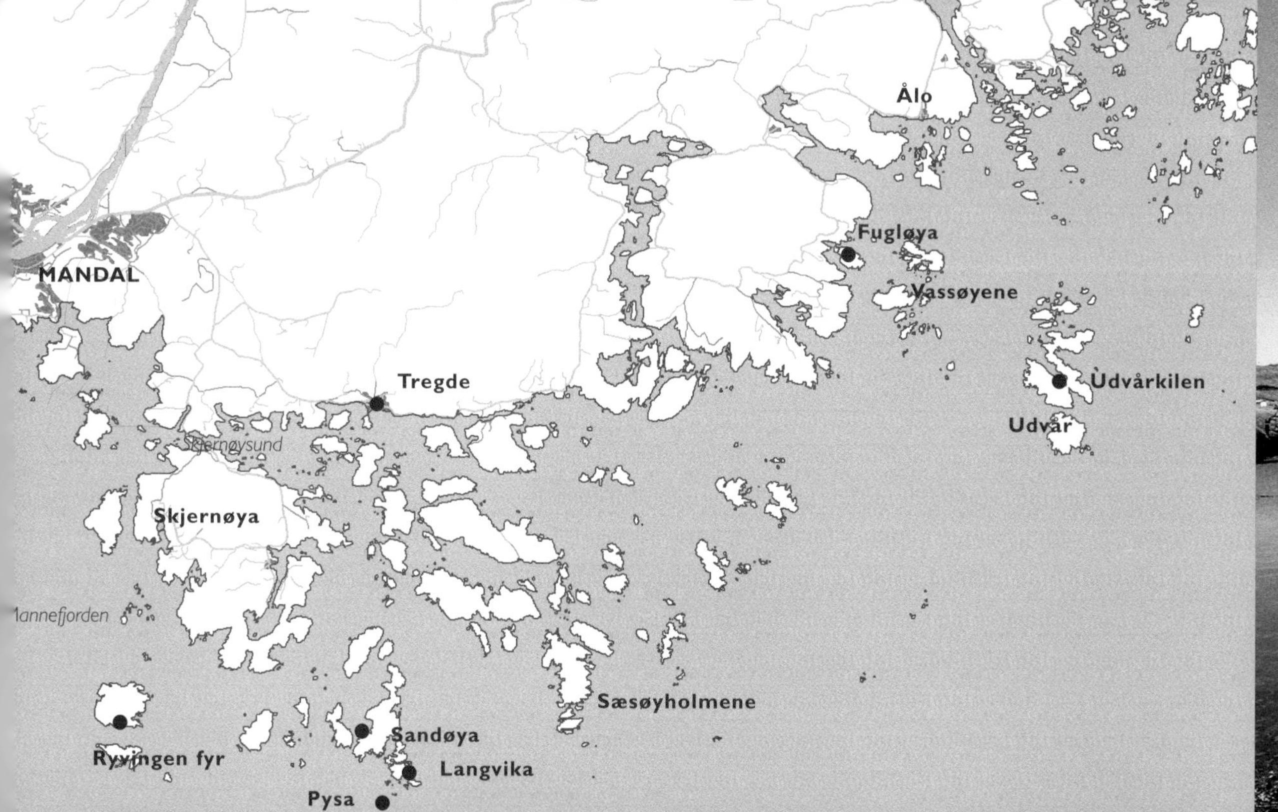

MANDAL

Mandal seen from Uranienborg, where you have a panorama view of the harbour and the archipelago.

The waterway to Mandal goes through the strait Skjernøysundet, which is clearly signposted and easy to sail. Far ahead, we see Sjøsanden and suddenly we are in Mandal, this cosy and charming southern town with a colourful history.

Timbre and salmon are the reasons why Mandal came into existence. It only acquired town status as late as in 1921.

The Mandal River has always been known as one of the best salmon rivers in the country. In the old days, salmon was an important trade. Mandal was called "the Danish Stalls" in those days, because traders from Flensburg and Southern Jutland had acquired privileges for trading, and also because large shipments of fish, game and berries were sent from Mandal to Denmark.

Today, again there is plenty of fish in the Mandal River and many enthusiastic sport fishers try their luck in the idyllic Salmon River.

The town is divided by the river and the white houses are an important part of the town's characteristic.

In the town centre, you find narrow streets and alleys in between old, well-kept whitepainted houses.

The Mandal church, from 1821, is one of the

Sjøsanden

Sjøsanden is one of the finest beaches of that region. It is part of the natural parks of Mandal, which consist of more than 250 acres of recreation area. Sjøsanden is only five minutes walk from the centre and must be seen – particularly if you are travelling with children, because the eight hundred metres long beach is shallow and perfect for children.

If Sjøsanden becomes too big and lively, you can walk through Furulunden to Risøbank where there are small, undisturbed sandy beaches in every bay and inlet. If it is windy, you will always find a spot shielded from the wind.

Earlier, these areas were open sand plains. In connection with the recultivation of the Vestnes plain, the idea was put forward to plant a belt of trees to stop the sand from moving.
Scotsmen were hired to help, and the Scots brought with them thousands of pines and larches. In the years between 1905 and 1935, hundred thousand plants were planted in the area.

country's largest wooden churches with 1800 seats.

Mandal is also known as the childhood home town of the brothers Emanuel and Gustav Vigeland, and their house is now a museum with stimulating exhibitions.

The town has a friendly and harmonious atmosphere, and even on busy summer days the tempo is just so. But if you are in Mandal on the second weekend in August, during the Shellfish Festival, the mood is continental. The town fills with visitors and it literally steams and bubbles everywhere.

From Mandal

The archipelago west of Mandal is exactly as wide and just as fine as the one on the east side of the town, all the way down to Hille. It has plenty of space and tempting harbours: Aspholmen just off Mandal and Risøbank is a good alternative to the guest harbour in town. Steinsøy is part of the Coastal Archipelago Park.

Furthest out is Mannevær, a fair-weather island, because it is very exposed. There are fine camping sites and bathing spots, and if you get cold, there is a cave with a door, concrete floor and a fireplace!

The waterway westwards past Hille is well sign-posted. The only thing that is lacking are holiday boaters. It seems like people believe that sailing to the southern coast down to Kristiansand and New Hellesund, or even to Mandal, is far enough, and they don't dare venture further west, not even to go round "Neset," as the locals call Lindesnes. There are after all limits!

Much of the archipelago disappears after Hille, and the coastline is more exposed and open, all the way to Lindesnes Lighthouse.

Hille

The island Hille southwest of Mandal is quite an experience. There are many good anchoring spots both on the east and west side of the island. But these are mostly fair-weather harbours, whether you choose Vestre Dansviga with easterly wind or Hillevågen with frisky westerly wind. Grunnesund and Vrageviga south of Meavraodden in Hille are great places with bedrocks and fine beaches.

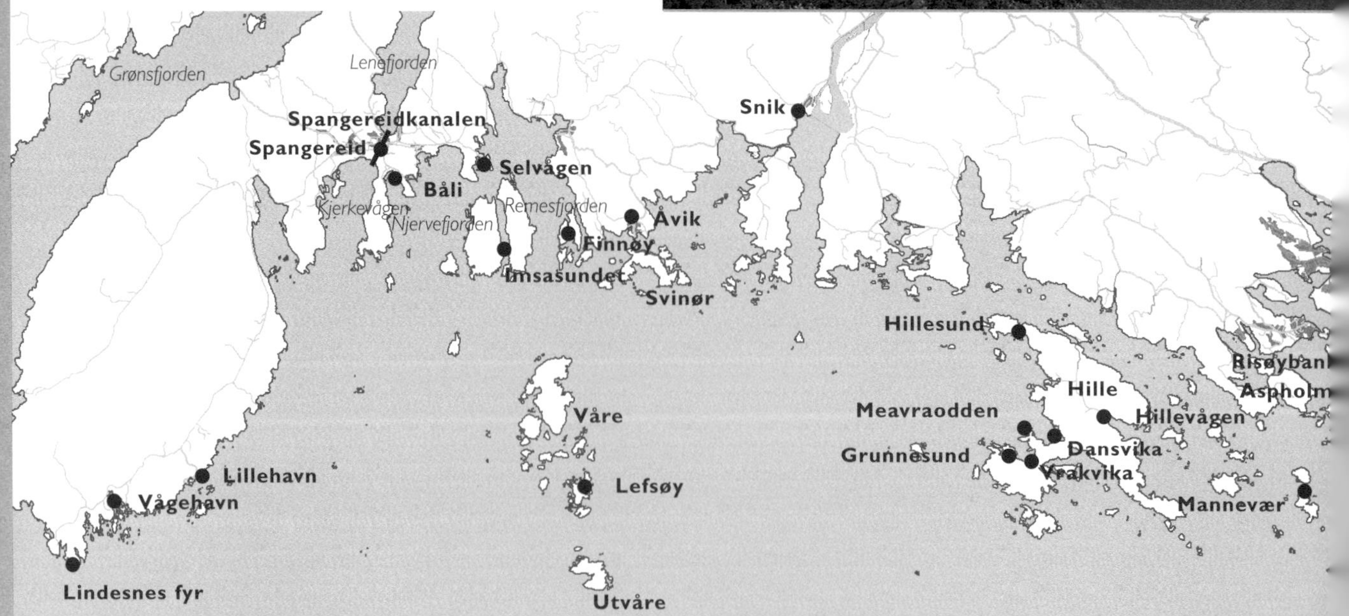

– and Round Lindesnes

Våre is a popular group of islands to visit before sailing round Lindesnes. Lefsøy, south of Våre, has a heavenly lagoon where you can moor safely, sheltered from the wind from most directions. North of Våre are the twin islands Imsa.

Lillehavn is a small fishing harbour straight to the south east of Lindesnes. Also Vågehavn is a fine little harbour just before Lindesnes.

If you choose to take the inner route via Svinør and Finnøysundet, you come to some idyllic places, well protected from the enormous sea. Continuing through Finnøysundet over Remesfjorden, you come to Selvågen and Båli in Njervefjorden.

New Bålihavn at the inner end of Kjerkevågen is the entrance to Spangereid Canal, which from the summer of 2007 helps boaters avoid the extremely windswept and unpredictable Lindesnes. The one kilometre long canal ends in Lenefjorden, and from there it is an easy route almost all the way to Farsund.

For more information see:
www.spangereidkanalen.no

Spangereid Canal
From the summer of 2007 you can take the shortcut to Farsund through the Spangereid Canal

Svinør (left) and Lillehavn (under).

Lindesnes

To sail around Lindesnes is considered by many people as an enormously daring venture. We won't go so far as to call it an extreme sport, because sailing on open sea is mostly about playing along with the wind and the weather. However, a pleasant trip tin good weather can quickly turn into a nightmare in storm.

In good weather it all looks so easy. Lillehavn is there peaceful and quiet. The glass dome on Lindesnes lighthouse sparkles in the sun. One hour later, you are past it and safely in the waterways of Korshavn.

In storm however, the sea outside "Neset" (the headland) is notorious. Nowhere else in Sørlandet does the sea rise as quickly, and nowhere else are the currents as dire. Around Lindesnes, it is important to respect the sea.

Lindesnes lighthouse is the oldest in Norway. It was built in 1655, and the first light was lit in 1656. Povel Hansen, Norway's first lighthouse keeper, received this private privilege.

Today, the unmanned lighthouse is a magnificent place, both in calm weather and storm. Under the lighthouse, an eight hundred square metres hall with auditoriums and exhibition halls has been built by blasting through the mountain. The new lighthouse museum makes the place even more attractive for visitors, which is dominated by car tourists, because there are not many seafarers who stop in the lighthouse harbour.

Lindesnes lighthouse is Vest Agder's largest tourist attraction, second after Dyreparken, the Kristiansand Zoo. Lindesnes is also the county's millennium place.

The lighthouse harbour
At Lindesnes Lighthouse there is of course a small harbour. The harbour is just outside the lighthouse, but is no port of refuge because it is too hard to sail to.
In good weather, however, without much undertow, it is fairly easy to get in to the harbour.

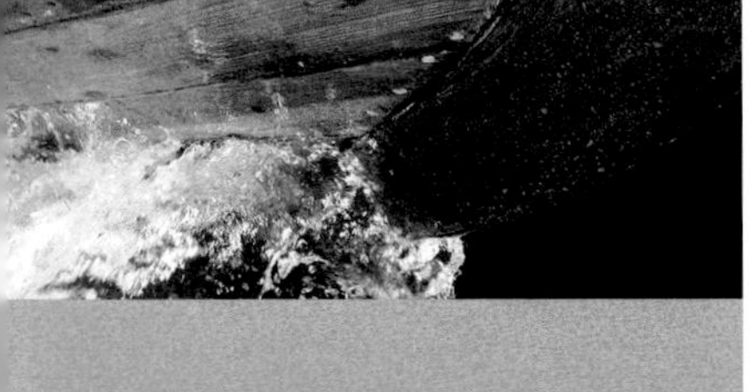

West of Lindesnes

When Lindesnes is safely behind us, we once again enter sheltered waterways. You can choose to sail in Grønsfjorden or head on to Korshamn. On the way, you pass Seløya whith a narrow, sheltered harbour.

Korshamn is a busy harbour, often used by both fishing boats and holidaymakers. It has rich traditions and in the last few years has become known for organising fishing for tourists. At most, there are over one hundred visitors and many of them are enthusiastic German sport fishers.

The discussion has been going on for a long time in the local community, whether it is the German tourists, the cormorants or the professional fishermen who are emptying the fjord of fish. Therefore, cod fish is being set out to boost the numbers.

In many ways, the coastline outside Farsund does not bear any resemblance to either Sørlandet or Western Norway. All the way out there is the archipelago, as it is further east, but closer to shore the cliff sides of the islets and rocks are extremely steep. We are not in Sørlandet anymore, but have not quite come as far as the Western County (Vestlandet) – we are in Southwest Norway.

From Korshamn the route continues to Farsund. It can be tempting to drop in at Spindfjorden which is sheltered and fine.

In good weather, you can venture all the way out towards Farsund archipelago in the waterway between Ullerøy and Langøy. But if the weather is shifty, it is better to seek out one of the many other sheltered mooring spots, for example in Skarveøy, where you will find many welcoming places to stay overnight, both on the west and east side of the island. Similarly, we can also recommend Skudevig on the east side of Langøy.

To get to Farsund town, you have to keep to a north-westerly direction towards west Langøy. Keep going in the direction of Katland Lighthouse. From there on, it is straight ahead to Farsund. But don't forget to make a visit to the buccaneer islands Loshavn and Eikvåg. These are truly the last gems of Sørlandet before the West County takes over with its rugged landscape and more modest houses.

The weather off the shores of Lista can be rough, but when it is good there are many fantastic places to visit. One of the most charming islets for bathing in this area is Hummerdus west of Einarsneset.

Diving

Korshamn Diving Centre is part of the Korshamn Tourist Centre Rorbuer. This area is exciting both for diving and sport fishing. You can dive in a kelp forest, do cave diving and explore old canons and shipwrecks. The surrounding waters have the densest concentration of shipwrecks, and the unique thing about them is that they are relatively untouched and therefore have the exciting lure of new discoveries.

KAV062

Katland lighthouse

Privateer Harbours

Loshavn and Eikvåg were Privateer Harbours during the Napoleonic Wars. Privateering was a major enterprise in these areas. The business was profitable, and generated great wealth for the skippers who had permission from the Danish King to arm small vessels with canons and raid English ships.

In the period between 1807 and 1809, hundred and sixty six so-called "letters of marque" were issued to Norwegian vessels.

The proceeds of the rather profitable privateering that ensued was often used to build and embellish private property in the ports to which the prizes were taken and the spoils divided up.

Loshavn

Loshavn with a wiew to Einarsneset in the horison.

Loshavn and Eikvåg

The outer harbours were built because the shipping industry needed easily accessible harbours outside the narrower waterways of the towns. Loshavn is not a big harbour, but it is stately with the beautiful terraced houses of the skippers. The fisheries, pilotage and cargo shipping were the biggest sources of income and these were owned by the Lund Company.

The Lund Family from Farsund built the biggest and most stately house in Eikvåg. They also owned the biggest house in Loshavn. Lund Company was mostly involved in cod fishing in the North Sea, and processing the fish as dried salt cod.

The stately houses of the skippers in Eikvåg and Loshavn are clear proofs that some people made good money during the Napoleonic Wars. The officers and the crew were recruited from Loshavn and Eikvåg, and they lived well off the shipping trade. Some used their wealth to build houses, which today comprise the central built up area in Loshavn.

Those who lived in Loshavn had good economy, and liked to flaunt it. They dressed up when they went to town. But the citizens of Farsund did not consider the people from Loshavn as better than others and they smiled at the Loshavners.

For most people, the war years 1807-14 were times of crisis and shortage of food as a result of the English blockage of grain import. Whether the rumour that people in Loshavn were so well off that they used castor sugar instead of sand on the floors in their houses is based on envy or fact is difficult to verify.

The pilot boat "*Veiviseren*" (the Pathfinder) from Eikvåg got twenty-three prizes during the war. This vessel alone got more than all the other privateer vessels together in Norway. The values were said to be equal to the astronomical sum of 500 000 silver coins.

Eikvåg

Farsund has been Norway's largest seafaring town, if you count tonnage "per capita." In contrast to many of the other southern towns, Farsund continued to be an important shipping place also after the transition from sailing to steam ships. The town hall, Husan, was built by Jochum B. Lund, the tradesman, who is considered Farsund's "progenitor."

In modern times it is the aluminium industry, shipping and furniture production that have been the main sources of income.

Farsund has had an enormous makeover these last years. There is still a fish hall in Farøy, marina and docks, but a guest harbour has been built by the town centre, and on the former industrial islet where container and boats were built there is now a service centre, shops and a promenade. Just a few steps away from the guest harbour there is a marina.

The historical privateer play is the main attraction during the annual Kaperdagene (privateer days) in July. During that period, there is a lot of hubbub in Farsund, with culture, pirates and shopping.

Farsund is located towards Listal that resembles Denmark with European beach grass and white sandy beaches. Lomsesanden, which has fantastic sandy beaches, would undoubtedly have had Norway's finest bathing place if the water temperature had been higher and the wind milder. It is truly windswept there. But when the good weather settles, there is no finer place. Nothing can match the beaches of Lomsesanden and Einarsneset.

«Husan» – Farsunds Town Hall

Einarsneset has sandy beaches that resemble those we find in West Jutland in Denmark.

Lista

Sailing along the Lista waterways always entails a certain tension. On the way westwards from Katland Lighthouse the nature forces are conspicuous. The currents draw the boat and the skipper feels the forces of nature taking over. Sailors found out early that the solution was an inner route. For hundreds of years, from Listeid in Eidsfjorden, boats, freights and passengers have been transported on land between Eidsfjorden and Framvaren. In the old days, the boats were pulled by horses. Nowadays, they are drawn by tractor trailers over Listeid.

Lista resembles the Danish landscape

Lista is unlike all other parts of the Southern Coast, perhaps with the exception of Jomfruland. It almost looks as if a part of Denmark has broken off and drifted towards Norway, because there you find long sandy beaches, lush cultivated land, with towering sky and much wind. The light over the fertile farmlands by the sea is exceptional in all seasons.

Lista has traces of one of the first ancient settlements in Norway. You get the impression that the landscape is just countless relics such as house ruins, grave mounds and rock carvings. And indeed, there are grave mounds on every farm in Lista. In connection with the major excavations at Lundevågen, archaeologists have been able to retrace 8000 years old habitats. The Bronze Age and the migration eras were the highpoints of Lista, when its inhabitants thrived on farming and trade. Lista has the mildest climate and soil in all of Norway, and at that time it was even milder than now. Visit the Lista Museum established in 1921. The museum's collections located in the beautiful nature in Vanse, span over the whole period, from early Stone Age to our times.

Emigration

Many people from Lista chose to leave their homes to seek their fortunes in America in the period 1880-90. Many settled in Brooklyn where they created their own colony of Norwegians, and after a while also their own "Lista Avenue".

The special thing about the Lista emigrants was that many of them chose to return after achieving their "American Dream." Therefore we still find many American words and styles of architecture and American cars in Lista.

Lista Lighthouse

Lista Lighthouse is more than a lighthouse. It is a remarkable landscape of stones, sea and sky. From a distance, it looks barren and uninviting. But closer inspection reveals a landscape full of life, plants, animals and birds. Lista Lighthouse is a bird station, an information centre, art gallery and lighthouse.

Lista Lighthouse has more than twenty thousand visitors each year. It was built in 1836, carved in granite and thirty six metres tall.

In 2003, the last lighthouse keeper left his post. Today the lighthouse is protected as a cultural monument, but still sends out powerful blinks automatically every fourth second.

88 ST
CC 77077
RUTEBILGARDEN
8th AVENUE
Bar & Supper CLUB
Varnes fyr
Eidsfjordenen
Framvaren
Jøllestø
Penne
Lista fyr
Borhaug
Vanse
FARSUND
Lundevågen
Eikvåg
Loshavn
Einarsneset

Jøllestø

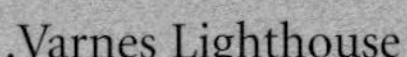

.Varnes Lighthouse

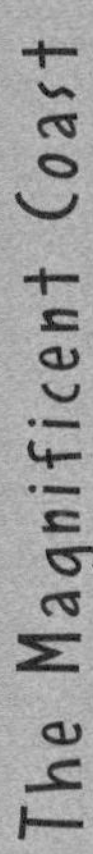

Towards Flekkefjord

The area around Lista is susceptible to storms. The North Sea is right out there and the waters are full of underwater rocks and unpredictable currents. The waters are almost always rough, irrespective of the wind direction, and it is therefore vital to keep your distance to the shore. Only after you go round Varnes Lighhouse by Listafjorden you can access the sheltered waters of the archipelago, first of all the big islands Hidra and Andabeløy. Southwest of Hidra you find a charming bay called Ytre Kalven, a fine sheltered place to moor, but difficult to enter if the sea is rough.

Rasvåg on the south side of Hidra resembles the many idyllic villages along the coast of Sørlandet. Small motorboats can use the Eide Canal that connects Rasvågen to Hidrasundet.

Kirkhamn is a big village west of Hidra, with busy fish halls, particularly during the mackerel fishing season in summer.

Eide Canal

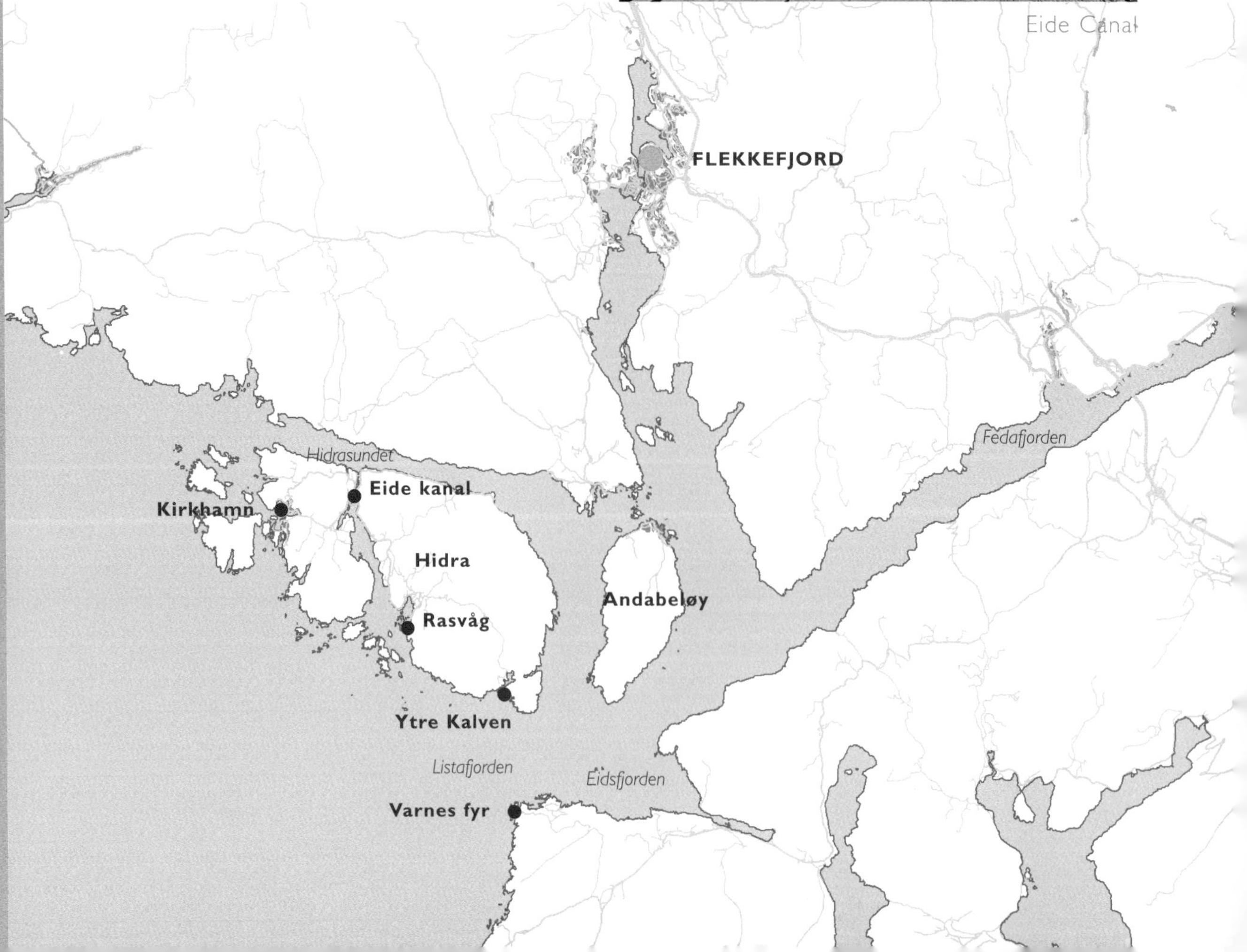

Open Sea

On the route from Farsund to Flekkefjord there are no archipelagos to seek refuge in for protection, before coming to Hidra. These waterways were among the most awesome coastal routes in the sailing ship era. History tells us about many tragedies. Several hundreds shipwrecks have been registered in the area. Many sailors hurry past Lista and its surrounding sea, and breathe out in relief when they arrive in calmer waters.

The boat route to Flekkefjord past Fedafjorden. We recommend a little detour in Fedafjorden to Feda, where seafarers always have sought a safe haven. Feda was for a long period the accepted place of assembly (Tinget).

Flekkefjord is the most westerly town in Sørlandet.
The town has one of the most beautiful entrances of the Southern Coast. It is narrow and spectacular but not difficult to navigate.

FLEKKEFJORD
Fedafjorden
Hidrasundet
Eide kanal
Kirkhamn
Hidra
Andabeløy
Rasvåg
Ytre Kalven
Listafjorden
Eidsfjorden
Varnes fyr

Varnes

Kirkhamn
is a sheltered place west of Hidra. The church is built right by the water and is the first thing seafarers observe when they approach the harbour, and the last thing they see as they head towards the open sea.

Feda

At the point where the coastal landscape opens up like an oyster you will find the "cultural pearl" Feda. This fishing village, all the way inside Fedafjorden, has some of the best preserved buildings in Vest-Agder County.

In "Bøkkerbua," you can follow the building of barrels step by step until the finished product, and you can buy one as a souvenir from Feda.

Feda is a pleasant beach located between hills and mountains all the way in Fedafjorden at the mouth of the river Fedaelva. Ever since the Viking era, seafarers have found a peaceful haven here, between Farsund and Flekkefjord. The place has also been an administrative centre for many hundred years. The old king's route crossed the fjord from Feda to Rørvik. And one of Norway's first post offices was built here in 1650.

"Head for Fedafjorden. The best place to stop is in the bay by the church on the west side of the fjord. You can moor there in calm waters, safe from the waves," wrote Paul Lövenörn in a map book from 1801. This sheltered harbour were well known to sailing skippers from Scotland, Holland and Germany. But already in the seventeenth century, the Dutch skippers found their way to Feda. With their broad, flat-hulled ships they could go all the way up Feda river to load oak timbre. This was among the most sought-after goods at that time, and was traded in for grains and clothes.

The extensive herring fishing, early in the nineteenth century, created the need for barrels in which to salt and preserve herring. In Feda, many people ventured on barrel production. The art of making barrels is called cooperage, and until the 1960s large numbers of barrels were produced in the cooperages along the river Fedaelva.

Along the fjord you see yellow and red houses, and seemingly each house has its own sea stall.

Around the church there are buildings with typical architecture

Hidra

Hidra is situated at the point where the southern coast meets the western coast. The archipelago is beautiful and has promises of adventures both below and above the surface of the surface. Hidra and the archipelago surrounding it have much to offer also on land, such as rich fauna and flora. Not surprisingly, this particular archipelago was protected in 2005.

Hidra is the largest island in Vest-Agder, about fifteen kilometres long and wide, and has around six hundred permanent residents.

Many summer guests have gradually discovered the uniqueness of Hidra, and during summer its population increases considerably. Nevertheless, it is never stressful in Hidra, because the island is big and offers a variety of activities for all tastes.

Hidra is actually two islands Austøya (East Island) and Vestøya (West Island). In between you find the Eie Canal which was officially opened on 13 October 1963, and allows a safer and shorter passage from the village Rasvåg to Flekkefjord. If you are not arriving by boat, you have to use a ferry to get to Hidra. An intense lobbying is going on to have a tunnel built to connect the island to the mainland.

Two dynamic local communities

The two villages Kirkehamn and Rasvåg are vibrant local communities, each in its own way. Kirkehamn has Hidra Church majestically located in the centre, all the way down by the sea, and a fishing harbour and trawler workshop in full activity. Rasvåg, where originally the old pilotage started, has characteristic and idyllic wooden buildings. The houses are built so close that their corners had to be cut in order to make way for cars.

Where the West Country begins

According to the local people, Hidra is where Sørlandet ends and Vestlandet (the West Country) begins. It is a good description, because there you find a combination of the idyllic landscape of Sørlandet and the rugged features of the West Country.

A paradise for divers and sport fishers

The conditions off the coast of Hidra are perfect for diving. The kelp forest is lush with fresh and fertile flora and fauna. Shipwreck divers can contact Hidra Diving Club for information and advice.

The distance from Hidra to the verdant kelp forest is short. There you find big cod fish, sandy bottom with flounders, coalfish and pollock grazing in the currents. The whole area by Hidra is full of fish and rather challenging.

Fish farming and crabs

The deep fjords, the regular water temperatures and the good currents around Hidra are ideal for salmon fish farming. This has become an important source of income in the last 15–20 years. When poisonous algae kill the fish in the nets, it is of course a crisis. It happens from time to time, but the people of Hidra never give up.

The Hidra crabs are famous. If you are in Hidra during the annual shellfish festival, you must visit the fishing harbour and taste the crabs, they are fabulous.

Rasvåg

The proximity to the sea is the reason why the area has acquired many impulses from Europe. Ships that went by Lista often had to wait for better weather conditions in the safe harbour at Rasvåg.

The view from Langeland Mountain is beautiful. You can see all over Hidra and its surrounding islands. From there it has always been easy to determine the condition of the sea and whether the journey could continue.

Kirkhamn

Hågåsen – Hidra

FLEKKEFJORD

Shipping has always been important to Flekkefjord. Already in the middle ages, the place had contact with the continent. Particularly the sea route between Flekkefjord and Holland was busy. The Dutch discovered early that the coast was a rich source of oak woods and stone. Already in the sixteenth century, timbre was freighted to Holland for shipbuilding and the construction of harbours. In Holland, they also needed stones for building their towns. Some say that Amsterdam is built on poles and granite boulders from Norway. Because of the good trading routes between the two countries, many youngsters headed off to Holland. Some stayed, while others returned with new impulses from the continent.

«Hollenderbyen» – (The Dutch Town), the built up area facing Grisefjorden, has narrow streets, well preserved small houses and sea stalls with obvious legacies from the Dutch era in the town's history. Apparently it was the Dutch who taught the Norwegians to eat lobster, and to catch them in traps rather than with pegs. There must have been enormous amounts of lobster in those days. The Dutch sent out special "lobster buses" to transport thousands of live lobsters to Europe.

The North Sea herring, the so-called silver of the sea, turned Flekkefjord into the leading harbour for export of salted herring, in Norway during the 1820s and 1830s. The local community prospered in this period and the standard of living improved. Admittedly, the herring had also earlier been a source of income, but the resources then were unreliable. However, the herring adventure came to a sudden end, and in 1839 it was over. After a short break to think things over, the industrious inhabitants of Flekkefjord began to examine new opportunities. But even today, fishing and particularly fish farming is still an important source of income for the community.

Flekkefjord acquired town status in august 1842, which ended the obligatory town tax to Kristiansand. The tanneries became the new trade, followed by wool, wood, barrel production, shipping and mechanical industry.

The battery at Grønnes on the east side of the fjord towards Flekkefjord was part of the coastal guard, which protected the town during the war with England in 1807–1814. The area is now used as a public recreation area and beach. The canons are only used for salutes in connection with the National Day and royal visits.

Flekkefjord museum is also worth a visit. The main building has been the home of a captain and a tradesman. The oldest building is from 1724, where you will find many examples of the cultural impulses that the Flekkefjord inhabitants received through their trade with Europe and particularly Holland, whether it was art, tools, textile or fashion.

Purple foxglove is Flekkefjord Municipality's flower

A street in the Dutch town

SØRLANDET
– the Magnificent Coast of Southern Norway
ISBN 978-82-92496-56-5
ISBN 978-82-92496-35-0 (Norwegian edition)

Photo:
© Alle photos by Øystein Paulsen, Jan Atle Knutsen and Øivind Berg except:
© Per Eide; page 74, 76, 83, 84, 93, 98.
© Erling Svensen; page 36m, 85b, 120/120, 123, 271bl
© Stein Bjørge; page 4
© Kerstin Mertens/Samfoto; page 138
© Pål Hermannsen/NN/Samfoto; page 50/51, 53
© Stein Johnsen/Samfoto; page 62, 100, 113
© Steinar Myhr/NN/Samfoto; page 114
© Tore Wuttudal/NN/Samfoto; page 160
© Øystein Søbye/NN/Samfoto; page 164
© Baard Næss/NN/Samfoto; page 165
© David Shale; page 95rm
© Tore Moy; page 149b
© David Nielsen; page 169mr
© Flødevigen archive; page 124bl

l=left, r=right, t=top, m=middle, b=bottom

© Illustration page 48: IMR
Maps: Authorisation code. NE14647-090606, source Statens kartverk

Kom forlag as
post@komforlag.no
www.komforlag.no
Publisher: Svein Gran

Translation: Caroline Babayan

Art director: Øivind Berg
Jacket design: Øivind Berg
Jacket photo: © Øystein Paulsen

Repro: Øystein Paulsen

Printed in Norway, PDCTangen 2007

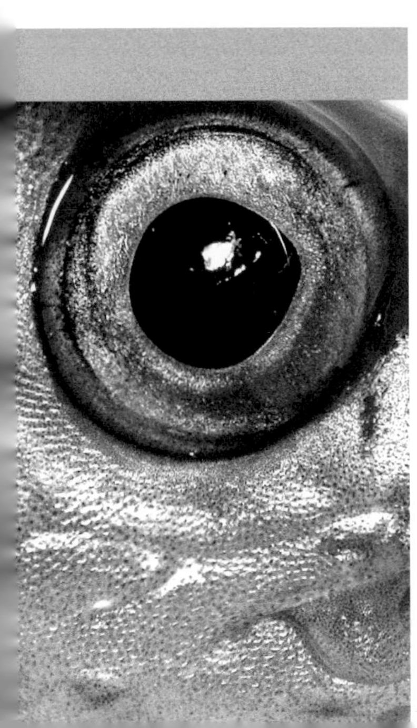

We would like to thank our contributors who gave us economic support in advance:
The County Governors of Telemark, Aust-Agder and Vest-Agder, the County Municipality of Aust-Agder, the County Municipality of Vest-Agder, Ministry of the Environment, Norway, Norwegian Coastal Administration, region Arendal, The Institute of Marine Research, and the municipalities Arendal, Kristiansand and Lindesnes.
We would also like to thank publisher Svein Gran, Kom Forlag, who ventured on this book project. It has given us security and peace to work.

We are grateful to all the departments and institutions that have kindly provided information on a variety of subjects such as: administration of land, waterways, cultural activities, marine biology, maps.

Special thanks to geologist Lars Kullerud, who has enthusiastically given us advice about the subject matters to be included in the section about geology. We are also indebted to attorney Frode A. Innjord, for reliable information about the history behind the creation of the Coastal Archipelago Park.
Svein Bjørnstad has piloted us through the archipelago from Langesund to Farsund. He has generously shared his many years of experience as "boat vagabond" along the Southern Coast.
And a greateful thanks to all of you we have met on our countless photo trips along the coast, who have kindly posed as models upon request.

Finally, we would like to thank our families, our employers and good colleagues for their patience, help and encouragement.
You have all inspired us.